CULTURES OF THE WORLD®
KOREA

Jill DuBois

BENCHMARK BOOKS

MARSHALL CAVENDISH
NEW YORK

PICTURE CREDITS
Cover photo: © Stephanie Maze/CORBIS
AFP: 34 • R. L'Anson: 13, 38, 39, 87 • APA: 5, 12, 27, 36, 40 (bottom), 52, 57 (bottom), 59,
65, 68, 103, 122, 129 • Art Directors & Trip: 6, 36, 44, 47, 49, 52 • Bes Stock: 1, 5, 8, 18, 46,
78, 94, 112, 122 • Camera Press: 43 • Corbis: 30 • Embassy of the Democratic People's
Republic of Korea: 40 (top) • Embassy of the Republic of Korea: 34 • Han Ka Ram Korean
Restaurant: 130, 131 • Hutchison Library: 23, 24, 25, 26, 32, 51, 60, 64 (top), 66, 67, 76,
83, 92, 95, 98, 117, 118, 126 • Image Bank: 3, 15, 19, 30, 33, 54 (top), 56, 62, 86, 89 • B.
Klingwall: 6, 9, 16, 17, 20, 22 (top), 29, 31, 37, 57 (top), 58, 64 (bottom), 69, 91, 105, 127
• Korean National Tourism Corporation: 4, 7, 10, 11, 14 (both), 18, 22 (bottom), 53, 54
(bottom), 61, 70, 72, 74, 75, 77, 78, 79, 80, 81, 82, 84, 93, 94, 96, 97, 99, 101, 102, 104, 107,
108, 109, 110, 111, 112, 113, 114, 115, 116, 119, 120, 125 (both), 128, 131 • Life File: 43,
123 • B. Sonneville: 1, 55, 90 • Travel Ink: 58, 86, 104

ACKNOWLEDGMENTS
Thanks to Marilyn Slaughter for her expert reading of this manuscript.

PRECEDING PAGE
Korean children enjoy a day out at the Olympic Park in Seoul, South Korea. Completed
in 1986, the Olympic Park contains sports facilities used in the 1988 Olympic Games,
and a fortress believed to have been built in the third or fourth century A.D.

Marshall Cavendish
99 White Plains Road
Tarrytown, NY 10591
Website: www.marshallcavendish.com

© Times Media Private Limited 1996, 1994
© Marshall Cavendish International (Asia) Private Limited 2004
All rights reserved. First edition 1994. Second edition 2004.

Originated and designed by
Times Books International, an imprint of
Marshall Cavendish International (Asia) Private Limited,
a member of the Times Publishing Group

Library of Congress Cataloging-in-Publication Data
DuBois, Jill, 1952-
Korea / by Jill Dubois.— 2nd ed.
   p. cm. — (Cultures of the world)
Includes bibliographical references and index.
ISBN 0-7614-1786-9
1. Korea—Juvenile literature. I. Title. II. Series.
DS902.D83 2005
951.9—dc22   2004007678

Printed in China

7 6 5 4 3 2 1

CONTENTS

Fish drying on bamboo.

Downtown Seoul.

INTRODUCTION

A DIVIDED COUNTRY, Korea looks forward to reunification. The Democratic People's Republic of Korea, or North Korea, is governed by communist ideals, while the Republic of Korea, or South Korea, is a democratic nation. Thousands of Korean families have been separated since the Korean War in 1953. Kim Dae Jung, the former president of South Korea, initiated the Sunshine Policy in 1998—talks aimed at building closer cooperation between the two Koreas. His presidency gave some South Koreans an opportunity to visit long-lost relatives in North Korea. That milestone gave birth to hopes among Koreans for reunification.

Perhaps the most poignant reminder of the Korean War is a statue in South Korea of two young Korean soldiers locked in an embrace. The statue represents two brothers' chance meeting on the battlefield while defending their own Korea. Though divided by ideological differences, Koreans look forward to the day when the border between the Koreas falls, and a new future as one nation begins.

GEOGRAPHY

THE KOREAN PENINSULA reaches southward from the neighboring nations China and Russia, into the East Sea, or Sea of Japan. The peninsula is located approximately between the same latitudes as the area between South Carolina and Vermont. Korea is surrounded by water on three sides: the Korea Bay and the Yellow Sea to the west, the Korea Strait to the south, and the East Sea to the east. There are more than 3,400 islands along the coast.

The Korean peninsula consists of two political units, the Democratic People's Republic of Korea in the north and the Republic of Korea in the south, which are divided by a line 38 degrees north of the equator. North Korea occupies 55 percent of the peninsula's 84,402 square miles (218,600 square km) of land.

Korea's name comes from the Goryeo dynasty, which ruled the peninsula from 918 to 1392. The name Goryeo means high and clear—an appropriate description of the high peaks and clear streams that characterize Korea's terrain. Korea is also often called the Land of the Morning Calm for its pretty and peaceful sunrise scenes.

Above: **Sunrise over Todam Sambong—the Three Peaks of Todam —in South Korea.**

Opposite: **Clear water amid fresh foliage in a mountain area in Korea.**

7

TOPOGRAPHY

Korean terrain is dominated by highlands. In North Korea, the Kaema Plateau covers land in the center and east, while the Hamgyong Mountains extend northeast.

Korea's highest mountain, Mount Paektu, is located in the region of the Hamgyong range, near the Chinese border. The extinct volcano contains a large lake in its crater, 9,003 feet (2,743 m) above sea level.

Smaller ranges in North Korea include the Kangnam Mountains, which stretch across the northwest, and the Nangnim and Myohyang ranges in the center.

The Taebaek Mountains, which extend into South Korea, include Geumgang, the only mountain in North Korea that can be reached from South Korea. Geumgang is 5,377 feet (1,638 m) tall and is famous for its scenery, as is Seorak (Snowy Peak), in the South Korean section of the Taebaek range. Seorak's highest peak, at 5,604 feet (1,708 m) above sea level, divides the mountain into the eastern Outer Seorak and the western Inner Seorak.

The Sobaek Mountains are located farther south. On Jeju, the largest island of the Korean peninsula, is South Korea's highest peak, Halla, at 6,398 feet (1,949 m).

RIVERS AND CRATER LAKES

Many of Korea's rivers are short and fast and drain into the Yellow Sea. North Korea's longest rivers begin at Mount Paektu and flow along the border with China. The Yalu courses 491 miles (790 km) west and drains into the Korea Bay, while the Tumen runs 324 miles (521 km) northeast and drains into the East Sea.

The Imjin flows 158 miles (254 km) into South Korea, where it meets the 319-mile (514-km) Han, South Korea's second longest river after the 324-mile (521-km) Naktong. The Naktong and the Han are tapped to supply water for industry and irrigation.

Korea's most famous lakes are volcanic crater lakes at Mount Paektu and Mount Halla. There is no volcanic activity on the peninsula, but there are hot springs and mineral springs. Many believe that the waters cure or prevent ailments such as indigestion, eczema, and rheumatism.

Left: **The sentinel-like Chongun, or Thousand Soldiers, cliffs line part of the Yalu's course.**

Opposite: **Hikers take in the view at Seorak's Flying Fairy peak.**

Jeju's smooth sands make it a popular island holiday destination.

ISLANDS

The Korean peninsula has many natural harbors on its southern and western coasts. There are beaches where streams enter the sea. The east has few beaches, because mountains line the coast.

More than 3,400 islands surround the Korean peninsula, mostly off the southern and southwestern coasts. Apart from the development of fisheries during the 20th century, life for the islanders has remained relatively unchanged for centuries.

Jeju, Korea's largest island, is located approximately 60 miles (95 km) south of the peninsula. Jeju has a population of half a million. Its wealth comes from fishing, citrus fruit farming, and tourism. Tourism is one of the island's biggest sources of income. With palm trees, beaches, caves, casinos, and golf courses, the island hosts more than 3 million tourists each year. Its residents live in a matriarchal society dominated by women spirit mediums.

CLIMATE

The Korean peninsula has a temperate climate and experiences four seasons every year. Monsoon rains make summer hot and wet, while winter is cold and dry.

During summer, from mid-June to mid-September, heavy monsoon rains account for nearly 70 percent of the peninsula's annual rainfall. In South Korea, summer temperatures range between 75°F and 85°F (24°C and 29°C). This kind of weather supports rice cultivation.

North Korea's summers are cooler: the average temperature is 68°F (20°C). The north also receives less rain annually—between 24 and 40 inches (60 and 100 cm)—than the 40 to 55 inches (100 to 140 cm) that the south receives.

The fall, from mid-September to mid-November, is Korea's shortest season. Frost first appears on October nights. Days are often pleasantly clear and crisp, with temperatures ranging from 55°F to 65°F (13°C to 18°C). The dry weather enables rice crops to ripen and be harvested. Winter crops such as wheat and barley are planted during the fall.

Winter, from mid-November to March, is not as severe in the south as in the north. Snow accounts for only 5 to 10 percent of the annual precipitation in South Korea, and rice and barley can be grown during winter. North Korea experiences bitter winters, with temperatures that range from 21°F to -8°F (-6°C to -22°C), the lower extreme being typical of the northern interior.

Spring, from April to mid-June, is short, when the snow thaws and rainfall increases.

Winter snow coats an ancient temple and its surroundings in Korea.

ELIXIR OF LIFE

Ginseng, or *insam* (in-SUM), is Korea's oldest export product. It is believed to be a cure-all, capable of improving a person's health in many ways, from increasing the appetite and mental powers to enhancing one's love life. Studies have confirmed the effectiveness of ginseng as a general tonic, producing positive effects on the central nervous system.

The consumption of ginseng dates as far back as 3000 B.C. The herb grew abundantly in Mongolia, northern China, and Korea. Its popularity in Korea led to overharvesting, and it grew scarce about a thousand years ago. To keep up with demand, the southern provinces began cultivating the herb. Ginseng continues to flourish in South Korea, today the world's leading ginseng root producer.

To cultivate ginseng, growers plant seeds in a mixture of oak and chestnut leaves in long rows of thatched shelters, away from sunlight. The seeds take between four and six years to grow into ma-

ture adults. Once harvested, the roots are washed, peeled, steamed, dried, and then sorted according to age and quality.

Korean ginseng comes in two varieties: *hong* (hohng), or red, and *baek* (back), or white. The white variety is less expensive and is readily available in Korea and throughout the world. It is believed to be adequate for general health if consumed regularly. The more potent red variety is especially useful to the elderly and people in poor health. Red ginseng is very expensive and is cultivated mainly for export.

Ginseng root may be dried or soaked, and packed in boxes or bottles (*above*). It is considered most effective when steeped in a liquid such as tea. A serious ginseng consumer completely submerges the root in tea and waits for the root's curative powers to seep into the tea before drinking. There are ginseng tea houses throughout Korea. Ginseng may also be used in the manufacture of commercial products, such as shampoo, or as a cooking ingredient to make porridge or soup.

FLORA

Korea's climate and terrain sustain large forests with a variety of trees. However, sections of the woodlands have disappeared. The Korean War caused defoliation; torrential rains cause erosion; and demand for fuel and timber cause deforestation. Major reforestation efforts have been implemented since the late 1960s. Tree species that will contribute to future timber needs are generally selected for planting.

Varieties of pine, maple, oak, poplar, birch, and willow are common in Korea. Fir, spruce, larch, and Korean cedar are abundant in the northern mountains. Reeds and sedges grow in stony lowlands that flood easily. The leaves of the rush plant, which grows in marshy areas, are woven into mats and baskets. There are also many endemic herbs, and herbal medicine is widely practiced.

Korea's flowering plants include camellia, forsythia, chrysanthemum, azalea, lilac, and rose. Azaleas, often depicted in Korean painting and poetry, color the hills bright pink in early spring. The national flower, called the Rose of Sharon, is a hardy hibiscus that grows again when cut off. The plant has a long growing season and symbolizes Korea's strength in adversity.

Fruit trees also flourish in Korea. Apples, pears, peaches, tangerines, persimmons, figs, and cherries are abundant. Native nuts include pine nuts, chestnuts, walnuts, and gingko nuts. In the warmer, subtropical climate of Jeju, bananas and pineapples are grown.

Weaving rush braids into a mat. The leaves of the rush plant are dried, then dampened to make them soft for braiding.

FAUNA

Animals found in Korea include badgers, bears, deer, leopards, weasels, wildcats, wolves, smaller mammals such as shrews, muskrats, and the Jindo dog, from the island of Jin, off the southwestern coast.

More than 350 bird species have been recorded in Korea. Cranes, crows, herons, magpies, orioles, robins, and swallows are endemic, while ducks, teals, swans, and geese are migratory.

The crane, often depicted in traditional Korean painting, is considered a symbol of good luck. The black-and-white magpie is a welcome sight early in the morning, as it is expected to bring good news.

CITIES

Korea's most populous cities are Seoul (11 million), Busan (4 million), Daegu (2.6 million), and Incheon (2.5 million) in the south; and Pyongyang (3.43 million), Hamhung (800,000), and Nampo (800,000) in the north.

SEOUL This metropolis on the Han River ranks as one of the 10 largest cities in the world. South Korea's capital serves as its

THE PALACES OF SEOUL

The spirit of the Joseon dynasty kings, who ruled the country for more than 500 years, lives on in Seoul, where the only palaces of Korea remain.

Korea's palaces are not single structures as are the castles of Europe. Korea's palaces are collections of buildings, interspersed with gardens and pagodas. They are generally modeled after palaces in China, with tiled roofs and sweeping eaves.

Three of the four palaces of Seoul are located in the northern part of the city. They were built facing south to catch the rays of the sun in winter and avoid evil spirits that were thought to blow in from the northeast. Behind them, the mountains served as a natural barrier to invaders from the north. The fourth palace is located in the center of the city and is much smaller than the others.

Seoul's palaces have been partially rebuilt over the years. They are a source of national pride, and the government plans to restore them to their original splendor.

political, economic, educational, and cultural hub. The city has been the capital since the Joseon dynasty, more than 500 years ago. Not far from the ultramodern hotels in the heart of Seoul are the ancient palaces. A 10-mile (16-km) wall was built around the city hundreds of years ago. There were nine gates in the wall, providing access into the city. Four of the gates were destroyed over the years.

BUSAN Busan is South Korea's largest port, its second-largest city, and the center of its fishing industry. With about 4 million inhabitants, Busan has tremendous industrial activity. Yet it remains one of Korea's most popular resort cities, with its historical landmarks, beautiful beaches, and hot mineral springs.

Opposite, top: **Cranes are a beloved bird in Korea. They are believed to bring good luck.**

Opposite, bottom: **The city of Seoul blends the new and the old.**

North Korean and United Nations guards at Panmunjeom stand on either side of the line dividing the two Koreas.

PANMUNJEOM Panmunjeom is the city where the leaders of the two Koreas hold talks to resolve economic and political disagreements. Of special significance is Panmunjeom's place in reunification talks.

The city is located on the western end of the north-south border, or demilitarized zone (DMZ). Once a farming village, Panmunjeom was obliterated in the Korean War. The DMZ is 2.5 miles (4 km) wide and stretches 152 miles (245 km) from the East Sea to the Yellow Sea.

Visitors can take bus tours from Seoul to Panmunjeom, except when reunification talks are underway. For many, the visit is a moving experience. Seeing the separation manifested so visibly emphasizes the degree of difficulty that the two sides face in trying to reach an agreement and reunite their people.

DAEGU South Korea's third-largest city is a major industrial hub, the nation's largest textile producer. Daegu is also a center for education. There are five colleges and four universities in the city.

Daegu is home to the Dalseong Fortress, built more than 1,700 years ago and now preserved in Dalseong Park. Daegu was once known as a market city specializing in apples and medicinal herbs. The city has adopted the eagle, magnolia, and fir tree as its symbols.

INCHEON   Incheon is located west of Seoul and is home to an international airport. With its beautiful beaches, the port city is popular among vacationers during summer. Incheon has a tidal range of 60 feet (18 m)—the second highest in the world. Nearby is Korea's fifth-largest island, Ganghwa, known for its historical sites.

GYEONGJU   This ancient city, the site of kings' tombs, pagodas, and Buddhist temples, is Korea's museum-without-walls. Gyeongju was the capital of the Silla dynasty, which flourished from 57 B.C. to A.D. 935.

In 1973 archeologists unearthed 11,500 artefacts from a Silla burial chamber, now called the Heavenly Horse Tomb, in Gyeongju. The thousands of historical treasures found in the Gyeongju valley have prompted the United Nations Education, Scientific, and Cultural Organization (UNESCO) to name the city one of the world's 10 most important ancient cities.

PYONGYANG   After being razed to the ground in the Korean War, most cities in North Korea were rebuilt with an emphasis on functionality rather than on architectural merit. North Korea's capital and financial center was the exception. Among its many landmarks are a modern subway, a sports stadium, and a 105-story hotel.

Pyongyang is believed to have been established as the capital in 2333 B.C. by Dangun, Korea's legendary founder. There is a mausoleum for Dangun in the city.

Pyongyang's Koryo Hotel is one of the city's most modern structures.

HISTORY

ANCIENT KOREA was called Joseon—Morning Calm. There are two legends explaining its founding. The first tells that a god-like figure called Dangun established the ancient state in the area that is now Pyongyang. He is credited with uniting the various peoples who inhabited the area around 2333 B.C. The Dangun era, known as Ancient Joseon, lasted more than 1,000 years. On October 3 each year, South Korea celebrates Dangun Day, also known as National Foundation Day.

Above: **Guardian statues at the Bulguksa Temple.**

Opposite: **The National Folk Museum in Seoul houses historical arti-facts, especially from the Joseon dynasty.**

The other prominent legend, supported in part by ancient Chinese texts, honors a Manchu tribal chieftain named Kija. According to the legend, Kija led a band of his supporters to Joseon after the fall of the Chinese Shang dynasty around 1100 B.C. He and his Manchurian successors then ruled the conquered territory until 194 B.C.

Legend aside, archeologists have determined that some prehistoric peoples of the Altaic language group probably migrated to the Korean peninsula from Siberia, Manchuria, and Mongolia. These early peoples were hunters, fishermen, and farmers who practiced shamanism and worshiped the spirits of nature. Their system of beliefs has survived in Korea through five millennia.

A fourth- or fifth-century painting discovered in a tomb in Koguryo, North Korea, shows a hunting scene.

THE ANCIENT KOREANS

Neolithic (late Stone Age) peoples who entered the Korean peninsula possibly as early as 6,000 B.C. drove out the Paleolithic (early Stone Age) Asians who were already living there. It is believed that the new settlers were the ancestors of modern-day Koreans.

The cultural development of the early Koreans was influenced by developments in China. Chinese models of civilization shaped Korean society. In 108 B.C. the Chinese had a more direct impact when the Han dynasty established four territories in the northern half of the Korean peninsula. That event began Korea's recorded history.

In 75 B.C. the Koreans recaptured three of the four territories. The remaining territory, Lalang, remained under Chinese control. It was through the flourishing Chinese colony of Lalang that characteristics of Chinese civilization—such as the system of writing, ideas on religion, government systems, and the art of iron working—were transmitted to the Koreans.

THREE KINGDOMS

By the first century A.D. there were three Korean kingdoms. Silla was founded in 57 B.C., Goguryeo in 37 B.C., and Baekje in 18 B.C.

The kingdom of Goguryeo, geographically the closest to China, was formed when several peoples united in the northeastern region of the peninsula. Initially the most powerful of the three kingdoms, Goguryeo established its capital at Pyongyang.

The kingdom of Baekje was founded by peoples who migrated southward to avoid the aggression of warriors from Goguryeo. Eventually these peoples occupied southern Korea, establishing their capital near Seoul.

Silla, the richest and most cultured of the three kingdoms, established its capital at Gyeongju.

The three kingdoms adopted Buddhism. Visitors from China introduced Confucianism.

Territories controlled by the kingdoms of Silla, Goguryeo, and Baekje in the seventh century.

In A.D. 618 the Tang dynasty came to power in China. Its rulers were eager to expand their sphere of influence. Capitalizing on hostilities among the three Korean kingdoms, the Tang dynasty helped Silla gain control over the peninsula, hoping to eventually control the expanded Silla. Silla conquered Baekje in 660 and Goguryeo in 668, but then encouraged revolts in Baekje and Goguryeo and defeated the Chinese troops that were sent to quell the revolts. Eventually, China agreed to recognize Silla as an independent state.

Silla spread its cultural influence throughout the peninsula, which was finally united under one Korean government.

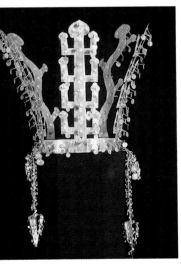

Gold ornaments from the Silla period reveal the skill of the Silla artists.

UNIFIED SILLA (668–935)

The Unified Silla period is often referred to as Korea's golden age of art and culture. Beautiful temples and shrines were built. The complicated Chinese writing system used in Korea was simplified, encouraging the spread of literature. Other forms of the arts also flourished, and Korea became a great Asian center for architecture, painting, music, and crafts such as ceramics, lacquerware, ironware, and gold and silver jewelry.

Artifacts that have been discovered among the remains of temples, tombs, and pagodas in Gyeongju, the capital of Unified Silla, reveal the remarkable accomplishments of the period. Some of these were the development of irrigation systems that improved rice cultivation, land reforms that benefited the poor, and the establishment of a national university. The economy boomed, as trade between East Asian nations expanded.

Unified Silla started to decline around 780 when infighting among nobles began. After many violent clashes, Wang Kon, the leader of a separatist faction, conquered Goguryeo, then Baekje, and finally Silla. In 918 he proclaimed himself the leader of a new state, with its capital at Songdo (present-day Kaesong, just west of Panmunjeom). Wang Kon called his nation Goryeo, a shortened form of the name Goguryeo, from which the name of Korea was later derived. A capable leader, Wang Kon was renamed Daejo, which means first king, after his death.

GORYEO (918–1392)

Korean culture thrived during the 11th century. Buddhism flourished through Goryeo patronage and became a powerful force in politics and culture. Buddhist scholars produced writings and art, and numerous temples and pagodas were built. Artists of the time also made valuable

celadon pottery and devised a form of poetry known as *sijo* (SAE-jo). A notable 11th-century Korean invention was moveable metal type. It had a major impact on the spread of literacy and culture, and came a whole two centuries before Gutenberg developed moveable type in Germany.

In the later Goryeo period, Confucianism grew in influence. The aristocrats professed Buddhism but looked to Confucianism for political and ethical guidance. Schools teaching Confucianism were built next to Buddhist temples.

The Choes were the successors of General Choe Chung-hon, who had established military rule in 1170. In 1231, during Choe rule, the Mongols invaded Goryeo. After 30 years resisting Choe rule, the people of Goryeo overthrew the Choes and concluded a peace treaty with the Mongols. Apart from occasionally interfering in Goryeo politics, the Mongols observed the treaty.

But by then, the Goryeo kingdom had other problems. Aristocrats owned most of the land, and some tenant farmers resorted to selling themselves as servants to pay the heavy taxes. Dissatisfied with the former Buddhist leaders, the government had recruited a team of neo-Confucian scholar-officials. It could not pay the new leaders well enough though, and they became disillusioned.

A new leader arose to meet the challenges facing the government. General Yi Seong-gye took over leadership of the kingdom in a peaceful coup in 1392 and founded the Joseon dynasty.

JOSEON (1392–1910)

General Yi realized that reforms were necessary if his reign was to be successful. He restructured the government and based it on Confucian concepts, emphasizing respect for elders and ancestors. Books on Confucian classics and literature were printed to encourage higher learning. Some of the ceremonies introduced in the dynasty are still practiced in Korea today.

Under Yi's rule, land was redistributed and Buddhist temples closed. The capital was moved to Hanyang (present-day Seoul), where Yi's dynasty, consisting of a small group of nobles, stayed for more than 500 years. Like Wang Kon, Yi was given the title Daejo after his death.

Sejong, the fourth ruler of the Joseon dynasty, showed tremendous concern for Confucian ethics. Class distinctions were firmly established during his reign in an attempt to create an ideal Confucian state. The importance of proper conduct between the individual and the family, and between the individual and the state were especially emphasized.

Sejong was considered the greatest Joseon king. His rule saw developments in technology, science, philosophy, and music. A major achievement was the creation of *hangeul* (HAHN-gool), a phonetic alphabet that could be used by the masses because of its simplicity.

Soon after Sejong's reign, the country fell under siege again. The Mongols presented a persistent threat at the border, and the Japanese raided the coast relentlessly.

THE IMJIN WAR

In 1592, Japan waged war on Korea. Under the powerful military leader Toyotomi Hideyoshi, Japan invaded Korea and conquered the cities of Busan, Seoul, and Pyongyang.

Homage being paid at the shrine containing the memorial tablets of the Yi dynasty kings. This ritual is performed on the first Sunday in May, in Seoul.

In 1598, after six devastating years of war, the Koreans finally forced the Japanese out with help from China. Were it not for the brilliance of Admiral Yi Sunsin, the inventor of an ironclad ship called a turtleboat, Korea's efforts might have failed. Farmland had been destroyed, and artisans and technicians captured and brought to Japan. The ravages of war and the loss of some of its finest minds left Korea a weak and unproductive state.

In the early 1600s, faced with Chinese aggression, Korea paid large amounts of money to avoid war. After its unfortunate encounters with foreign powers, Korea isolated itself from all nations except China, and became known as the Hermit Kingdom. But in doing so, Korean society stagnated while other nations experienced a rich period of intellectual achievement.

China kept its stranglehold on Korea until Japan defeated China in the Sino-Japanese War (1894–95). But in 1904 Russia fought Japan for Korea in the Russo-Japanese War until Japan's victory in 1905, which resulted in the Japanese annexation of Korea in 1910. A new, highly oppressive era began.

JAPANESE RULE

After Japan annexed Korea in 1910, Japanese citizens, helped by the new government, took over Korean businesses and landholdings. The Japanese exploited Korea's natural resources and built roads, railroads, ports, and dams, thus modernizing Korea.

However, Korean culture suffered. Koreans were forced to adopt Japanese names and to participate in Japanese religious rituals. The Korean language was prohibited from being taught to or even spoken by Korean students in schools.

Japan's oppressive rule motivated the historically complacent Korean people to stage demonstrations to gain international support for Korean independence. Major protests were held throughout the country in a united effort after the Korean delegation at the post-World War I Versailles Conference near Paris failed to gain approval for self-rule in 1919.

Japanese forces moved to quell the independence movement, called Samil. It is thought that as many as 7,000 Koreans were killed in the violence that ensued, and thousands others were imprisoned.

The entrance to the secret gardens where Korea's royalty lived until Japan annexed Korea.

KOREA DIVIDED

When the Allies defeated the Japanese in World War II, the Korean peninsula's fate fell into different hands. Caught in the Cold War, the United States and the Soviet Union worked to prevent each other from taking control of Korea.

The bridge at Panmun-
jeom connecting North
and South Korea.

The Soviet Union pushed for a communist government, while the United States insisted on a capitalist system. The two nations agreed that the Soviet Union would accept the Japanese surrender north of the 38th parallel, while American troops would stay south of the line until a plan was developed to reunite Korea. When, after two years, the two nations still could not reach an agreement on Korea's future, the United States turned the situation over to the United Nations.

The United Nations' solution was to give the Koreans the power to decide on the issue in a free election. But since the Soviet Union would not allow the UN Commission that was to oversee the election into the north of the peninsula, an election was held only in the southern half in 1948. Syngman Rhee won the presidency, the Republic of Korea was formed, and its National Assembly drew up a constitution. Shortly after, the Soviet Union announced the formation of the Democratic People's Republic of Korea, led by a communist general, Kim Il Sung. Both governments claimed to represent the whole country.

NORTH KOREA AND THE UNITED NATIONS

North Korea's relationship with the world community remained unstable after the Korean War because of its hostility toward South Korea. North Korean forces carried out several attacks on South Korean and UN forces in the DMZ. In 1968 North Korean troops invaded Seoul and made an assassination attempt on the South Korean president.

Korean ties seemed to be mending when in 1972 the two Koreas held talks that led to a reunification resolution. That resolve did not last long. North Korea soon resumed its attacks.

North Korea's international relations showed signs of improvement in the 1990s. With South Korea, North Korea became a member of the United Nations in 1991 and signed a joint denuclearization declaration in 1992. In 1994 North Korea signed an agreement to stop all nuclear activity. With its nuclear power plants shut down and its crops destroyed by flood and drought, North Korea faced fuel and food shortages.

The world community responded with aid, but in 2002 North Korea admitted that it had an active nuclear weapons program. UN inspectors in the country were forced to leave, and the nuclear facility at Yongbyon, north of Pyongyang, was reactivated.

Opposite: **Soldiers near Mount Paektu. North Korea has invested heavily in its military.**

THE KOREAN WAR

In June 1950 North Korean armed forces attacked South Korea in an attempt to unify the peninsula. The event marked the beginning of the Korean War.

American soldiers entered the war in September but were forced to retreat to the southeastern corner. Subsequently a UN force consisting of combatants from 16 nations was sent to support South Korea against North Korean aggression. The UN force moved into North Korea close to the Chinese border, when China entered the conflict in support of the communists. A stalemate resulted, with armies positioned at the middle of the Korean peninsula. A ceasefire was signed in July 1953.

The Korean War dealt a heavy blow on both sides of the 38th parallel. The North Korean population was drastically reduced, and cropland throughout South Korea was ravaged and Seoul nearly leveled.

Political differences keep the two Koreas apart. North Korea remains steadfastly communist, while South Korea is firmly capitalist. Yet, such opposing ideals have not crushed the hopes of 70 million Koreans for eventual reunification.

IN QUEST OF PEACEFUL REUNIFICATION

In 1972 the two Koreas jointly announced that they would open dialogue for peaceful reunification. During the next 20 years, tension grew between the two Koreas. Negotiations progressed at a painfully slow pace, sometimes with years between meetings.

Political observers have questioned the sincerity of North Korea's intended "peaceful reunification." Incidents of hostility have included North Korea's dispatch of armed ships into South Korean waters, the discovery of three tunnels dug by North Koreans under the demilitarized zone, the discovery by satellite of secret nuclear sites that generated suspicions of North Korean nuclear arms development, and the bombing of a South Korean jetliner.

North Korea, on the other hand, claims that the Team Spirit military exercises conducted by the United States and South Korea are not compatible with reunification dialogue.

What is the probability of reunification? For half a century, the two Koreas have followed opposing ideologies. Those skeptical of reunification point out that the north has laid down unacceptable preconditions for the form of government and the domestic and foreign policies of a unified Korea. Sobered by the strikes, unemployment problems, and high tax rates that characterized German reunification, South Korean reunification advocates now think that the process should not be rushed, as hasty reunification could set back South Korea's booming economy for years. In the meantime, as both sides continue to delay the process, the gap between the two Koreas continues to widen.

GOVERNMENT

NORTH KOREA AND SOUTH KOREA each have a president as their head of state. But while South Korea's president serves one five-year term, North Korea's president Kim Il Sung stayed in office from 1945 until his death in 1994, when he was succeeded by his son, Kim Jong Il.

THE CONSTITUTION

South Korea's constitution was adopted in 1948 and has since been revised nine times. The constitution allows for three branches of government: the executive, headed by the president; the National Assembly; and the judiciary. The South Korean president is elected for a single five-year term. He can appoint or dismiss the prime minister, with the National Assembly's approval, as well as ministers and heads of office. The president is both head of foreign relations and commander-in-chief of the armed forces.

Above: **A poster in North Korea promotes self-reliance. The words at the bottom read "Long Live the Great Juche Idea!"**

Opposite: **City Hall in Seoul.**

The North Korean constitution, adopted in 1972, promotes *juche* (CHOO-cheh), or self-reliance. North Korea has had to be self-sufficient, because its trade relations are restricted to communist or politically nonaligned nations. There are also three branches of government: the Supreme People's Assembly; the Central People's Committee; and the Administration Council, which is responsible for the ministries. The president is elected for a four-year term by the Supreme People's Assembly and may be reelected.

31

STUDENT PROTESTS

Following a tradition from the Joseon era, the nation's scholars have held the responsibility of being watchdogs of the government.

Since the state of South Korea was created in 1948, its students have represented the national conscience in matters of democracy and human rights. Their protests have often been effective. Student uprisings forced the authoritarian Syngman Rhee to resign in 1960 and the military government to write a constitution in 1987 that called for democratic presidential elections.

Unfortunately, student protests have sometimes turned violent. From the late 1980s to 1990 reforms were pursued as a substitute for riots. But in 1990, just when officials started to believe that riots might be a thing of the past, a student protesting a tuition hike was killed by riot police, sparking off violent demonstrations on campuses across the nation. Twelve demonstrators set themselves on fire. Since Kim Dae Jung began his administration, students have taken a more peaceful approach in organizing demonstrations.

GOVERNMENT

The National Assembly is South Korea's lawmaking body. Voters elect two-thirds of the members of the assembly for four-year terms. The remaining third are represented proportionately by political parties winning five or more seats in the election. Some of the functions of the assembly are: to propose, pass, or reject legislative bills; to ratify foreign treaties; to confirm or reject the appointment of the prime minister; and to oversee administrative agencies.

The most powerful body in the North Korean government is the Supreme People's Assembly. Voters elect its members to serve four-year terms. Some of its functions are: to formulate state policy; to approve legislation and the budget; and to elect the president, prime minister, Central People's Committee members, legal officials on the president's recommendation, and Standing Committee members, who vote on bills and amend legislation when the assembly is not in session.

ARMED FORCES

South Korea's military consists of the army, navy, air force, Marine Corp, and Coast Guard. There is also a reserve force of about 4.5 million, and military service is compulsory for men ages 18 to 28 for up to 26 months. South Korea's defense expenditure is slightly more than 3 percent of its gross domestic product (GDP).

In addition to the army, navy, and air force, North Korea's military includes 100,000 special forces troopers and reserve units consisting of a workers' army (called the Red Guards) of about 4 million members and a youth army (called the Young Red Guards) of about 1.2 million high-school students. Compulsory national military service, starting from age 17, lasts 10 years for men and seven for women. North Korea's official defense expenditure is about 23.5 percent of its GDP.

At attention in their smart navy uniforms, these men in white are among 50,000 who defend South Korean waters.

SOUTH KOREA'S ROAD TO DEMOCRACY

South Korea's first president, Syngman Rhee, promised to introduce democracy in the nation. But his weak and corrupt leadership led to nationwide student protests, forcing him to step down in 1960. In 1961 General Park Chung Hee proclaimed martial law. He later retired from the military and won the 1963 presidential election. Under Park's leadership, the constitution was amended to increase presidential power and freedom of speech and of the press were severely restricted. Park was assassinated in 1979.

The military then took over the government. Attempts to restore constitutional rights led to violent clashes between the military and demonstrators. In 1980 General Chun Doo Hwan, who led the military action against the demonstrators, took control of the nation. His presidency was marked by student demonstrations for the reinstatement of direct elections.

In 1987 Roh Tae Woo, a former general, won the presidency. Because he had been a major participant in the 1979 coup, many questioned his commitment to democracy. In 1992 Roh was replaced by Kim Young Sam. Kim introduced political and economic reforms, but his term was plagued by corruption. In 1998 Kim Young Sam was succeeded by Kim Dae Jung.

KIM DAE JUNG was branded a communist by Park for his liberal views on reunification, but he remained popular among the people. In his first presidential race, Kim won 46 percent of the votes. He continued his campaign against Park despite political persecution. In 1973 he was taken from his hotel in Tokyo by South Korean agents and held prisoner for days. He was released only when the U.S. ambassador intervened.

When Park was assassinated in 1979, the new president, Chun, imposed martial law and arrested Kim and other opposition leaders. The United States intervened, and Kim left for the United States in 1982. When he returned to Korea several years later, he was put under house arrest. Kim persevered through another two electoral losses before winning in 1997, at the height of the Asian economic crisis and at the age of 72. In 2000 Kim was awarded the Nobel Peace Prize for his contribution to the process of reunification.

LEADERS OF THE NORTH

A personality cult surrounds the two Kims of North Korea: the late president Kim Il Sung (called the Great Leader) and his son and successor, Kim Jong Il (known as the Dear Leader).

Kim Jong Il (*right*) was named his father's successor in 1980 and began preparing for the role from then. He was appointed to a key position in the Korean Workers Party. His position enabled him to remove party members who opposed his succession.

In 1985 Kim Jong Il's birthday was declared a public holiday. In 1993 he was appointed supreme commander of the military, a position traditionally held by the president.

Ambitious and intelligent, Kim Jong Il surrounds himself with technocrats who influence North Korea's economic strategy. Foreign analysts have called him a terrorist, identifying him as the mastermind of the 1983 bomb attack in Rangoon, Burma (Yangon, Myanmar) that killed members of the South Korean cabinet. Their accusation has not been conclusively proven.

POLITICAL PARTIES

The ruling party in South Korea is the Millennium Democratic Party. Its leader, Roh Moo Hyun, became the nation's 16th president on February 28, 2003, succeeding Nobel laureate Kim Dae Jung.

The main opposition party, the Grand National Party, holds 115 seats in the National Assembly. The third most prominent party, the United Liberal Party, holds just 17 seats.

Communist North Korea has one major political party, the Korean Workers Party. All other political organizations are affiliated with it, which leaves little room for opposition.

ECONOMY

SINCE THE KOREAN WAR, South Korea has played a major role in the global economy. Before 1960 there were few Korean industries that were developed and Korea had few natural resources on which to rely. The division of the peninsula into two independent states disrupted domestic trade patterns and left South Korea without access to mineral resources.

Despite such barriers, South Korea has grown into a global producer of steel, iron, automobiles, ships, and electronics. South Korea is the 12th largest economy in the world and the sixth largest trade partner of the United States.

The economic picture in North Korea is the reverse. At first, North Korea's economy grew rapidly because of available resources and the communist government's ability to marshal the people to work. When the economy became more complex, the government's rigid control of the economy lowered efficiency.

Opposite: **A busy street in Seoul, South Korea.**

Below: **A fishing town north of Wonsan on the eastern coast of North Korea.**

Today the North Korean economy is plagued by problems such as a lack of human resources. Losses suffered in the Korean War and the maintenance of large reserves of armed forces have worsened the labor shortage.

In the 1980s North Korea began to pursue joint ventures with foreign companies, achieving its first joint venture with China—a marine fishery products enterprise—by 1989. Attempts to acquire Western capital and technology have largely been unsuccessful.

Workmen at a dock in Busan.

INDUSTRIES IN SOUTH KOREA

MANUFACTURING accounts for 75 percent of industrial production in South Korea. Although nearly all of South Korea's industries are privately owned, there is often cooperation between the government and the private sector. Sometimes the government develops new industries and slowly privatizes them; other times it offers incentives to entrepreneurs to start new businesses. This cooperation between private business and the government has led to the rise of huge business groups, known in Korea as *chaebol* (JAE-bull).

One well-known *chaebol* is 45-year-old Hyundai, which consists of more than 20 companies producing automobiles, ships, furniture, and computer chips, among other things. Hyundai and South Korea's three other large *chaebol*—Lucky Goldstar (LG), SK, and Samsung—produce more than half of the nation's GDP.

In the last two decades, production of electronic goods such as television sets and computer chips has developed so significantly that South Korea is now a world competitor. Machinery and ships also play a major role in industrial manufacturing.

MINING South Korea's principal minerals include coal, gold, silver, tungsten, talc, and iron ore. With limited natural resources, the nation is developing overseas mining interests to meet its needs.

CONSTRUCTION A burgeoning economy has created a construction boom. Roads, buildings, and sewer systems are being developed to keep pace with economic growth. South Korean construction workers are also active in building projects abroad, particularly in Southeast Asia, the Middle East, Latin America, and Africa.

A tremendous construction boom has resulted from the economic development of South Korea.

INDUSTRIES IN NORTH KOREA

MANUFACTURING North Korea manufactures machinery for domestic industries, such as agriculture and the armed forces. Metal-cutting machines, tractors, weapons, and army vehicles are some examples of North Korea's products, but since the quality of the machines is often poor, the country also imports equipment from other countries.

MINING About 80 to 90 percent of the Korean peninsula's important mineral deposits, especially coal, iron ore, lead, zinc, tungsten, and fluorite, are found in North Korean territory. The main coal mines are located north of Pyongyang. More than half of the nation's electricity output is generated by coal-powered plants. Iron ore is a major export item, followed by steel, lead, zinc, and cement.

AGRICULTURE, FISHING, AND FORESTRY

SOUTH KOREA As recently as the 1950s, agriculture represented about 70 percent of employment. By the early 1990s, agriculture employed only 14 percent of South Korea's workforce. Despite the drastic drop, there are still some 2 million small farms, most of which are privately owned rice farms. Other South Korean crops include vegetables, soybeans, barley, and wheat.

South Korea is one of the world's leading fishing nations, with a fleet of more than 800 deep-sea vessels. Efforts have been made to expand the fishing industry. Fish is a major export commodity and is the main source of protein in the Korean diet. In addition to the deep-sea fleet, thousands of boats work the coastal waters, which contain an abundance of fish and shellfish.

NORTH KOREA Extensive forests of spruce, larch, fir, and pine on the mountain slopes of North Korea provide the nation with timber. North Korea also imports timber from Russia, because the local forests cannot meet the domestic demand on their own.

Farms are concentrated in the western plains, which make up only around 20 percent of North Korean terrain. The redistribution of land to

WHAT THE WORLD CUP DID FOR SOUTH KOREA'S ECONOMY

Co-hosting the 2002 FIFA World Cup with Japan improved South Korea's global presence and image. The event helped improve South Korea's product reputation, and demand for its exports grew. In a Korea Investment-Trade Promotion Agency survey of 10,188 foreign consumers a year after the World Cup, 66 percent of the respondents said that they had bought Korean products within the year. That was a significant increase from the 57 percent that had been recorded in a survey conducted immediately after the opening of the World Cup in Seoul. Reasons given for buying Korean products included quality, competitive pricing, design, and brand name.

The survey also revealed that although people have strongly associated South Korea with the World Cup since 2002, this association is slowly diminishing. In its place is the nation's growing reputation as a fast-developing economic superpower. Most of the respondents said that South Korea's most competitive industry was electrical and electronic products. Samsung was rated the nation's top company by 23 percent of the respondents, while 19 percent named Hyundai, 17 percent Lucky Goldstar, and 15 percent Daewoo.

The World Cup attracted soccer fans from around the world, but the Japanese, who make up the largest number of tourists in Korea, stayed in their own country to enjoy the World Cup. In spite of the drastic fall in the number of Japanese tourists in South Korea that year, however, an increase in the number of tourists from other countries and of Koreans staying home instead of vacationing abroad helped keep South Korea's tourism industry in balance.

the peasants after World War II divided already small farms into even smaller ones. The drive for collective farms intensified after the Korean War, and in the 1980s North Korea had nearly 4,000 cooperative or state-owned farms. Today, about 37 percent of the working population are employed in agriculture, and the two most important crops are rice and corn. Farms are well-equipped with ploughing, planting, transplanting, and harvesting machines.

In the 1980s North Korea launched a land reclamation program to expand its agricultural land. Construction of the West Sea Barrage was completed in 1986. The $4 billion project included a 5-mile (8-km) dam on the Taedong River. Believed to be the longest dam in the world, it provides water for fish ponds and farm and industrial use and also generates electricity.

Fishing is also important to the North Korean economy. The state has invested in large fishing ships and trawlers for deep-sea fishing in the Yellow Sea and the East Sea.

Opposite top: **The West Sea Barrage blocks the flow of the Taedong River, creating an artificial lake that sends water through canals to irrigate agricultural land along the western coast of North Korea.**

Opposite bottom: **Coastal villagers sort a fresh squid catch.**

UNDERSTANDING THE *CHAEBOL*

The idea of the *chaebol* was first introduced in the 1920s and 1930s when Korea was under Japanese colonial rule. The Korean *chaebol* was fashioned after the Japanese *keiretsu*. The government's plan was for economic development in Korea to benefit Japan. Several privately owned companies were set up in Korea, but the Japanese government strictly controlled their credit, applications for licenses, and other business measures.

When Japanese rule in Korea ended, the Koreans fine-tuned the processes and procedures of the *chaebol*. The effort was advocated by President Park Chung Hee, the president of South Korea from 1961 until his assassination in 1976. The *chaebol* concept encouraged the formation of conglomerates under a single holding company, usually controlled by a family. All the companies were essentially interlinked through holdings of one another's shares. Unlike the *keiretsu*, which have one large financial institution, the *chaebol* do not have their own financial institutions. They require the government's approval of financial backing since South Korea's banks are nationalized.

Much of the blame for South Korea's collapse during the 1997–98 Asian economic crisis fell on the influential *chaebol*. Under a 1998 agreement with the International Monetary Fund for economic aid, South Korea was to open its financial and corporate sectors to foreign investment. The Fair Trade Commission, formed by President Roh Moo Hyun, aims to investigate and restructure South Korea's family empires. The collapse of the multi-billion-dollar Daewoo was a lesson to the South Korean government to ensure that *chaebol* conform to legal processes.

TRANSPORTATION

Korea's transportation system is growing rapidly. Each state has a well-developed highway network linking major cities, and the capital cities have good subway systems. Bicycles are a popular form of recreation in South Korea but are virtually nonexistent in North Korea.

The state-owned freight and passenger railroad runs more than 1,950 miles (3,120 km) in South Korea and 3,240 miles (5,200 km) in North Korea. The train system is important in Korea's mountainous terrain, particularly in the north.

There are five international airports: Incheon, Jeju, Gimhae (Busan), and Yangyang in South Korea, and Sunan, just outside the North Korean capital. South Korea's Korean Air and Asiana Airlines and North Korea's national airline, Koryo, handle domestic and international flights. Koryo flies mainly to China and Russia.

THE KOREAN WORKER

Koreans have a strong work ethic. A recent survey revealed that work is second only to family in importance, and Koreans put in the hours to prove it. The average Korean in a manufacturing job works up to 55 hours a week, compared to the 40-hour week of the average factory worker in the United States.

Korean society is based on a deeply rooted hierarchical social system. Koreans' respect for superiors takes the form of polite observances, such as rising in their presence and not leaving the workplace before them.

The polite and gentle demeanor of Koreans in social interactions is different from the competitiveness and tough negotiation skills they demonstrate in business. Koreans also have a deep-rooted loyalty. A Korean would give a job to someone whose loyalty he or she values rather than a person who may seem more capable.

ENVIRONMENT

ENVIRONMENTAL PROBLEMS such as pollution come with industrialization. Air pollution is one of South Korea's major environmental concerns. Automobiles and industrial facilities are the main sources of pollutants, especially in the larger cities. The South Korean capital, Seoul, has one of the highest automobile ownership rates among the nation's cities—and ownership is growing.

Heavy industries cause severe pollution in areas where they are concentrated, especially if manufacturing plants do not take care in treating and disposing of chemical waste. Dumping has led to the spread of diseases such as cholera and dysentery.

Among the environmental consequences of population growth has been deforestation. Korea's forests have long been harvested for fuel. Deforestation has led to floods, droughts, and the loss of wildlife.

KOREAN COLLABORATION

To preserve Korea's natural environment, the governments of the two nations have established parks and reserves and initiated reforestation projects. Also, in a move toward improving bilateral relations, the two governments are making a joint effort to slow down environmental degradation in the demilitarized zone. Both sides have agreed to stop destroying trees in the area for surveillance purposes.

However, construction of the inter-Korean railroad and highway that will pass through the western part of the demilitarized zone has raised concerns about its potential impact on the rich ecosystem. Studies have shown the zone to contain over 2,000 species of plants and animals, including endangered or unrecorded ones. Rare species include eagles, antelope, cranes, frogs, and roe deer. South Korea aims to register part of the zone as a transboundary biosphere reserve.

Opposite: **A persimmon tree stands laden with fruit outside a house in the countryside.**

REFORESTATION Korea's reforestation programs conserve trees that have economic potential. Trees selected for reforestation tend to have short growing seasons; to be able to grow in the different climates of the different regions; and to be useful to the fiber, paper, and edible oil industries. Reforested areas help to control shifting sands and winds, moderate floods and droughts, and contribute to the lumber, furniture, food, perfume, and paint industries. The South Korean government has implemented two 10-year reforestation projects, in 1971 and 1984.

PROTECTED AREAS The Korean governments have set aside certain natural areas where human activity is restricted. These areas include

Korean rice farmers. More environmentally friendly alternatives to chemical fertilizers and pesticides include keeping fish in rice farms.

A walk across a mountain bridge gives a view of Korea's flora in autumn.

national parks and reserves throughout the peninsula. If part of Korea's demilitarized zone is eventually declared a transboundary biosphere reserve, the United Nations Educational, Scientific, and Cultural Organization (UNESCO) will grant North and South Korea financial and technical assistance in preserving the area.

In some farming areas in Seoul, the use of chemical fertilizers and pesticides is prohibited in order to protect the soil and water from pollution. The challenge for farmers seeking to achieve sustainable agriculture is to develop natural methods of soil fertilization and pest control even while increasing crop output.

POLICY AND AWARENESS   South Korea passed an Environmental Preservation Act in 1977. In the 1990s, the new environment ministry restructured and expanded the act. But the success of environmental policies and projects depends on the understanding and cooperation of the Korean people. Environmental preservation is taught in schools in South Korea in order to increase public awareness and participation,.

BATTLING AIR POLLUTION

While North Koreans face the most severe problem of air pollution in areas with concentrated heavy industry, South Koreans breathe poor air in large cities as well.

South Korea's environment ministry has taken serious measures to manage the quality of air in Seoul's metropolitan region. Efforts to deal with pollution in such a densely populated area have required close cooperation between the government and the people, and not only corporations but also individuals.

The Special Act on Seoul Metropolitan Air Quality Improvement was passed in 2003 to gradually reduce the level of pollution and clear up Seoul's skies. The act essentially puts the region under strict regulations to enforce the use of methods and devices that control emissions from automobiles and industrial facilities.

Two of the environmentally friendly inventions the South Korean government is promoting are low-emission cars and clean fuels.

LOW-EMISSION CARS do not depend solely on fossil fuels. They use alternative sources of energy, such as electricity, and release smaller amounts of hydrocarbons and toxic gases, such as carbon monoxide, which are produced by burning fossil fuels. Hybrid electric cars, for example, run on two energy sources: petroleum and electricity.

Low-emission cars are a relatively new concept among Koreans. To raise the rate of adoption of such cars, efforts aim to encourage the manufacture of low-emission cars and to stimulate domestic demand. While electric cars are environmentally friendly, conventional cars are convenient to refuel. Combining these benefits, hybrid cars offer a platform for South Korea's transition to newer fuels.

CLEAN FUELS Zero- and low-emission cars have not yet rendered conventional cars obsolete. To reduce their destructive impact on the quality of air in Seoul, automobiles that run on fossil fuels are being equipped with emission filters and more efficient engines.

South Korea is also exploring cleaner fuels. Natural gas, consisting mainly of methane, burns with hardly any smoke and releases far less ozone gas when burned than petroleum does.

Natural gas is used in Korea in power plants and in factories and households. The use of natural gas as a fuel has also been extended to various automobiles such as city buses in Seoul and Busan and even garbage trucks.

Particles suspended in the air form a suffocating veil over Seoul. Measures to reduce air pollution are expected to significantly reduce the occurrence of respiratory diseases in the city.

MILESTONES IN WASTE MANAGEMENT

The Korea Waste Management Network (KWMN) of South Korea was set up in 1997 to promote more environmentally friendly systems of household and industrial waste management. It bands together more than 250 nongovernmental organizations. The network played waste watchdog during the FIFA World Cup in 2002.

One of the KWMN's main aims is to reduce the use of disposable items and spread the use of reusable items in South Korea. Among its biggest achievements has been the successful recommendation that supermarkets and department stores be prohibited from giving out free plastic bags to their customers. Shoppers who want plastic bags have to pay for them.

The network established Korea's first no-disposables fast-food chain, Lotteria. With its pilot outlet in Seoul, Lotteria has led the way for other fast-food chains to replace disposable forks, spoons, cups, and burger boxes with non-disposable alternatives in order to cut down the enormous amount of waste generated by the fast-food industry every year. The KWMN is also urging supermarkets and manufacturers to use less packaging in their products.

The Korea Foam-Styrene Recycling Association (KFRA), a nonprofit organization, was established in 1993 to promote more environmentally friendly ways for Koreans to use expanded polystyrene, which has been listed as a recyclable material since 1996. Polystyrene used in packaging for electrical or food products, for example, can be recycled into substitute materials that can be used to make furniture or compact disc cases.

The KFRA provides national-level support for local governments in improving their recycling systems and increasing the proportion of expanded polystyrene that is recycled every year.

TOWARD A WASTELESS SOCIETY

While incinerators pollute the air, landfills pollute the land. The South Korean government has found that the best solution to the problem of waste is reduction.

Plans to make South Korea a wasteless nation include providing recycling companies with financial support and educating the public on recycling through pamphlets and media campaigns. Laws on the treatment of waste apply to products that become harmful to the environment when disposed of. Examples include food and beverage containers that are made from synthetic materials such as polystyrene and polypropylene.

To encourage households to recycle, a fee is charged based on the amount of waste generated by each household. Manufacturers are encouraged to use fewer synthetic materials to reduce their products' potential to generate waste from consumption. Manufacturers are also responsible for developing waste collection systems and recycling or treatment facilities.

Under Korean law, recyclable products and packaging should be clearly marked with a sticker to indicate to consumers that the materials can be recycled. Korea's recyclables list includes glass, certain plastics, steel and aluminum cans, paper, batteries, refrigerators, computers, car tires, air conditioners, and light bulbs. There should also be a collection system in the product distribution area to facilitate the movement of materials to the recycling centers.

Tin cans and plastic and glass bottles containing rice wine, beer, and other drinks can be recycled after consumption.

KOREANS

THE POPULATION OF KOREA is nearly homogeneous—nearly every inhabitant of the peninsula is Korean. A scant 20,000 Chinese living in South Korea make up the peninsula's largest minority group, and a few Japanese live in North Korea.

Koreans have great ethnic pride, and they strive to preserve a single identity. While there has been cultural contact between China and Korea throughout history, ethnic mixing has been rare. Having a keen awareness of cultural and ethnic differences has enabled the Korean people to retain their homogeneity. The concept of multi-ethnic nations such as the United States runs contrary to the Korean view of statehood. The ethnic Chinese living in South Korea are not citizens but residents holding Taiwanese passports.

Only since the Korean War in the early 1950s has there been some degree of ethnic mixing on the peninsula. During the war, many American servicemen and Korean women married and started families.

Opposite: **Three Korean teenagers hang out.**

Below: **An elderly couple in traditional clothing.**

OLD SOCIAL SYSTEM

During the Joseon dynasty, a hierarchical social system divided the people into different social classes and defined relations between them. The classes were determined by scholastic achievements and by occupation rather than by wealth. The social system also established an obligation to authority and deemphasized individual rights.

Class distinctions were abolished in the 1890s, but many descendants of the social elite still benefit from their status. Class distinctions can influence marriage arrangements, political affiliations, and employment opportunities.

YANGBAN The highest class, the *yangban* (YAHNG-bahn), were the power-elite. They included the scholar-officials and military officials, and their families. Only the *yangban* could take the civil service examinations that measured knowledge of Confucian ideas. Passing the examinations allowed them to hold government positions. If unemployed or poor, they were prohibited from doing more menial work, but they maintained the Confucian rituals and attitudes that made them figures of authority in their village.

JUNGIN Between the *yangban* and the common class were the *jungin* (JAHNG-in). As physicians, interpreters, handicraft makers, artists, and military officers, the *jungin* served as an important link between the common people and the *yangban*.

SANGMIN The *sangmin* (SAHNG-min), or common people, made up about 75 percent of the population. Consisting of fishermen, merchants, farmers, and minor administrators, this large class carried the burden of all taxation.

CHONMIN The lowest class was the *chonmin* (CHOHN-min), or despised people. They included slaves, servants, convicts, jailkeepers, shamans, actors, and entertainers.

Above: **Villagers, usually farmers, often belong to the lower class because of their poverty.**

Opposite top: **Farmers once belonged to the *sangmin* class.**

Opposite bottom: **Handicraft makers were once members of the *jungin* class, which mediated between the *yangban* and the *sangmin*.**

CONTEMPORARY CLASSES

A new class structure has emerged in Korea, and it is determined by wealth. Since the end of the Korean War, city dwellers in the south have grown richer because of industrialization and economic growth. These economically comfortable Koreans make up the new middle class that includes managers, healthcare professionals, and even factory workers.

The population of urban poor is decreasing. Most are recent arrivals from rural areas. Koreans of the lower class generally live in rural areas, eking out a living by farming. Education is the key to social mobility.

DRESS

Most Koreans in the cities wear Western-style clothing. Older Koreans, especially in rural areas, may wear traditional clothing. Many scoff at the modern fashions of city dwellers and take almost snobbish pride in wearing shabby, old-fashioned clothes. In the north, people everywhere wear military uniforms. During festivals, however, most Koreans wear traditional clothing when they take part in ritual celebrations.

The traditional Korean dress is called the *hanbok* (HUN-bok). It is loose-fitting for cool comfort and beautifully detailed with colors. The *hanbok* for men consists of bloomer-like pants called *baji* (BAH-ji), a short sleeveless jacket or vest, and a coat called a *durumagi* (doo-roo-mah-gi). The *hanbok* for women consists of a short jacket or blouse called a *jeogori* (JUH-go-ri) and a long skirt called a *chima* (CHI-mah). The *chogori* has a long sash tied in a bow on the side.

The modern design of the *hanbok* is quite similar to styles that were worn during the Joseon dynasty. There are different types of *hanbok* for different occasions, such as the Lunar New Year, first and 61st birthday celebrations, and weddings.

There are some rural areas in Korea where grandmothers, or *halmoni* (HALH-muh-ni), and grandfathers, or *haraboji* (HAH-rah-buh-ji), wear traditional clothes every day and look like their ancestors in old photographs. An old man will typically have dangling amber buttons on his jacket, rubber shoes with pointed, upturned toes, and a tall hat, or *satkat* (SUD-cut), woven out of black horsehair. Old men in rural areas often have long braided hair that is knotted on top of their heads.

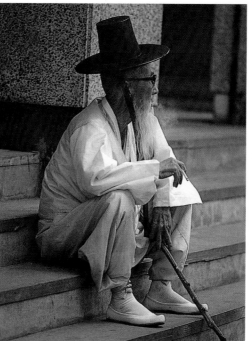

Above: **Casual attire is the norm in Pyongyang, North Korea's capital.**

Left: **An old man wearing the traditional tall black hat and pointed rubber shoes.**

Opposite: **Two women in traditional dress, called *hanbok*. It consists of a long skirt and a short jacket, with a bow tied on the side.**

LIFESTYLE

KOREAN THOUGHT AND BEHAVIOR have been influenced by centuries-old philosophical and religious ideas. While economically modern, Koreans cling to many of the ways of living that their ancestors followed.

Every aspect of Korean society, from housing to education, from gender roles to friendships, has a Confucian slant, a slight Chinese influence, and a very identifiable Korean flavor.

CONFUCIANISM

Confucianism is not a religion. Based on the ideas of the Chinese philosopher Confucius, Confucianism is a social and ethical code of behavior and the first organized way of thinking to be accepted in Korea.

Above: **Participants in a Confucian rite honor the Chinese sage.**

Opposite: **Two girls stop for a drink at a vending machine in Gyeongju, South Korea.**

Unlike a religion, Confucianism does not involve the worship of a higher being. But like some religions, it attempts to guide human relationships and improve social and ethical conduct. As such, it is an all-encompassing philosophy on lifestyle. The fundamental thrust of Confucianism is to maintain peace and order. It has rules for familial relationships that emphasize harmony. It stresses the importance of education and respect for authority.

The five relationships considered most important in Confucianism are father/son, ruler/subject, husband/wife, elder/younger, and friendship. Koreans are very conscious of proper behavior and the loyalty of friends.

Three generations pose for a photo in a park. It is common to see extended families enjoy their leisure time together.

FAMILIES AND CLANS

The Korean family structure is part of a larger kinship structure that is defined by specific obligations. The kinship system has four levels.

HOUSEHOLD   The ideal Confucian family has four generations under one roof. Multigenerational households are quite common in rural areas in Korea, but urban families may not follow this pattern. Young married couples start their life together in an apartment away from their parents.

The Confucian household is made up of husband and wife, their children, and the husband's parents if he is the eldest son. This arrangement is called *jip* (jip), meaning big house. The households of younger sons are called *chagunjip* (CHAH-gehn-jip), or little house.

In a Korean home, the head of the family—usually the oldest male—holds the position of authority, and every family member is expected to do as he says. There is an understanding that the authority figure will always be fair in dealing with members of the household. According to Confucian ideals, the authority figure also represents, supports, and protects the family. Should he be unable to do this properly, he will lose face as the family head.

Respect for authority, a valued virtue in Confucianism, is what maintains order in traditional Korean families. In the ideal Confucian household, the wife obeys her husband, the children obey their parents, younger siblings obey their older siblings, and so on according to the family hierarchy.

MOURNING GROUP The second level of the Korean kinship system, the *tangnae* (THANG-nay), is made up of people who have the same ancestry going back four generations on their father's side. The *tangnae* gathers at graveyards to perform rites that offer respect to ancestors.

A *tangnae* performing ancestral rites.

LINEAGE The third level, *p'a* (pah), is the lineage that traces all the descendants of one man. Thousands of households may belong to one *p'a*. A *p'a* is not only responsible for performing ancestral rites; its members also provide aid for needier members of the group and oversee the behavior of younger members. A *p'a* often owns land and buildings, such as gravesites and schools, that its members can use.

CLAN The highest level is the *tongjok* (THONG-jok). *Tongjok* members have the same surname, or family name. This group is so large that it generally does not have great feelings of solidarity. The most practical function of the *tongjok* is to determine the acceptability of marriage partners. There are strict rules against marrying someone who shares a common ancestor on the father's side, no matter how far back. There are only about two hundred family names, and hence as many *tongjok*.

DEVOTION TO PARENTS

Filial piety is a child's sense of complete devotion to his or her parents. Koreans feel a strong sense of gratitude and obligation toward their parents, most intensely a man toward his father. In Confucianism, filial piety is considered even more important than a subject's observance of respect for his ruler.

Dedication to one's elders is considered an essential factor in the formation of one's personality. It is part of the idea that the family, or group, is a more important unit in the framework of society than the individual. The application of filial piety is extended in Korean society beyond parent-child relationships. It is a code of behavior relevant to interactions with all elders.

FRIENDSHIP

Loyalty between friends is also very important in Korea. Friendship is one of the few equality-based relationships in Korean society. When two people become friends, they expect to stay friends for the rest of their lives.

For Koreans, most friendships date back to their schooldays—the time in most Koreans' lives when their peers are truly their equals. Within a group of boys or girls, there are no status markers to differentiate students. Each is involved in the same experience. Friends are expected to be there in

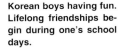

Korean boys having fun. Lifelong friendships begin during one's school days.

THE CLAN DILEMMA

South Korea bans intra-clan marriages. The age-old ban makes it very difficult for couples who check their family trees only after falling in love and deciding to get married. The ban has affected some 300,000 couples who cannot register their marriages and are thus considered not legally married. People in intra-clan marriages cannot claim tax exemptions for their spouses, and their children are technically considered illegitimate. Some couples emigrate to get their marriages legally recognized.

COPING WITH THE BAN The South Korean ban on intra-clan marriages originated in China. According to Confucian scholars, the ban was imposed to prevent birth defects, which were believed to result in babies from marriages involving close relatives.

To avoid intra-clan matches, major clans maintain offices that keep extensive genealogical records. The oldest recorded Korean ancestry, the Gimhae Kim clan, dates back to A.D. 42, nearly 2,000 years ago. While such impeccable record-keeping is admirable, it also restricts young Koreans from following their hearts.

OPPOSING THE BAN There is compassion in South Korea for the plight of intra-clan couples, even on the part of the government. Twice in the last 15 years, the National Assembly declared a one-year suspension of the ban on registering intra-clan marriages. Nearly 5,000 marriages became legal during the first amnesty period, and more than 12,000 during the second. In 1996 couples from the same clan were allowed legal marriages if they had lived together since at least the year before.

China and North Korea have abolished their laws prohibiting intra-clan marriages, but two sections of South Korean family law still uphold the ban. Feminists and legal experts believe that the total abolition of the ban is in South Korea's future. For a nation that wants to be viewed as modern, the cancellation of this prejudicial law that focuses solely on the father's bloodline is probably just a matter of time.

times of need to support and to help solve problems. To deny a friend's request is unthinkable.

As one's friendships mature, they extend from one's personal life to include one's professional life as well. Friends are expected to provide contacts and opportunities to one another throughout their careers. In 1987, for example, a great political debate centered on President Chun's intention before retirement to ensure that all members of his graduating class of the military academy had suitable civil-service posts so they would be taken care of in their retirement years.

Top: **A young worker in a South Korean printing plant.**

Bottom: **A train guard in North Korea.**

ROLE OF WOMEN

Korean society is male-dominated. Korean women traditionally hold subservient positions. Few pursue careers. The woman is considered an "inside" manager, who tends to home matters. She is the homemaker, raising the children, monitoring the household finances, and doing the daily chores. If her husband's parents live with them, she takes care of them as well as she does her husband and children.

Koreans traditionally prefer sons to daughters. In traditional Korean culture, a son carries the family line and takes over the family business, while a daughter marries into another family and bears children for that family. Even today, Korean families deciding to send their children to international schools or abroad for a Western-style education almost always send their sons rather than their daughters.

Much traditional Korean culture still forms a big part of present-day Korean society, although economic demands have changed things to some extent. The contribution of women has been essential to the tremendous economic success of South Korea. The nation's work force includes nearly 9 million women. Yet working women in South Korea do not enjoy the same rights as their male counterparts. Many hold low-level jobs in export-oriented industries and work long hours for low wages. However, as more women acquire a college education, more go into professional fields such as education, medicine, law, and business.

Women in South Korea are fighting for better working conditions by legal means, especially through the National Committee of Women's Policies and the Korean Women's Development Institute, both created in 1983 through a presidential decree. The Korean Women Workers Association United, founded in 1992, develops campaigns to improve the status of women in the workplace.

HAENYEO—WOMEN OF THE SEA

In South Korea, where traditionally women stay home to take care of the household and their family, Jeju, an island just south of the mainland, counters the norm.

On Jeju, it is traditionally the women who go out to work while their husbands stay home. *Haenyeo* are a dwindling group of women who dive for sea urchins, abalone, and octopus in the deep, frigid waters off the island. They continue a tradition that goes back more than 1,500 years. It is a grueling, backbreaking vocation that has been passed down from mother to daughter.

Haenyeo dive for up to four hours a day in summer and about 15 to 20 minutes in winter, when the temperature of the water can plummet to about 50°F (10°C). They dive without scuba equipment. They stay submerged for around two minutes at a time and make shrieking noises as they release oxygen upon completion of a dive.

Before the invention of wet suits, female divers were the natural choice because women had more layers of fatty tissue beneath their skin than men did and could thus be better protected against the cold of the water.

The *haenyeo* tradition has since continued on Jeju, and the divers have long been the symbol of the island and the subject of folk songs, sculpture, and souvenirs. However, the divers of Jeju are a dwindling community. There were about 24,000 *haenyeo* in the 1970s, but only a few hundred are left. They once ranged in age from 20 to 70 years, but those left are more than 50 years old. Modern women have chosen to break tradition rather than follow in their mothers' footsteps, because deep-sea diving the *haenyeo* way is a difficult and often debilitating job. The greatest problem that the divers suffer is the effect of water pressure on their ears and sinuses. Many go deaf after years of diving, while others become addicted to painkilling medications that they use to fight off discomfort.

While the *haenyeo* appear to enjoy economic independence and greater autonomy than their mainland sisters, they are obliged to contribute one-fifth of their income to a fund that supports the many unemployed men of their villages. The rest of their money goes to husbands and sons, so that they can make the major financial decisions.

MALE-FEMALE RELATIONSHIPS

In early Korean society, men and women were segregated and had little opportunity to interact with the opposite sex and develop social skills involving the opposite sex. Although Korean men and women are now freer to mingle, old practices such as matchmaking are still common. Dowries continue to play an important role in Korean marriages and involve large sums of money and family business mergers.

Marriages were not viewed as equal partnerships until recently. The relationship between husband and wife was traditionally not a close friendship. Instead, marriages were based on the wife's respect for and obedience to her husband, who was considered the superior in the relationship. As the modern Korean woman takes her place in society, however, the traditional relationships are slowly giving way to greater equality and friendship.

KIBUN AND NUNCHI

Visitors to Korea are often surprised to learn of the importance of *kibun* (KEY-boon), or harmony, in interpersonal relationships. Some have remarked on the apparent disregard Koreans have for strangers on the street. Koreans do not have the same concept of personal space as Westerners do, and the natural shoving and bumping come across as rudeness to foreigners accustomed to more space.

Kibun can be harmed by a number of etiquette blunders, such as reprimanding a worker in the presence of others, not showing due respect to a superior, using one's left hand to pass something to a superior, or saying something negative about a person's hometown. To Koreans, preserving proper *kibun* is essential to accomplishment. If a person is hurt or loses pride in the course of reaching a goal, the project is considered a failure.

Maintaining *kibun* is a complex process. In seeking to preserve a harmonious and comfortable emotional climate, individuals have to consider the state of mind of people around them while keeping a satisfactory state of mind themselves.

Sensing the emotional pulse of others calls for another Korean way of thinking, called *nunchi* (NOON-chi). *Nunchi* is an intuition, or hunch, that helps one read another's state of mind. People who can easily judge the body language, tone of voice, and general demeanor of other people are better able to preserve *kibun* and social harmony.

The wife's traditional relationship with her husband is based on obedience.

South Gate Market in Seoul. Crowds are common in South Korea's large cities.

INTERACTIONS WITH STRANGERS

Foreigners who have visited Korea are often surprised to learn of the importance of *kibun*, because visitors always remark on the apparent disregard that Koreans have for strangers. Koreans live comfortably in crowded conditions, as they do not have the same concept of personal space as Westerners do. The unintentional shoving and bumping that Koreans find natural to encounter in the street may appear as rude behavior to foreigners who are accustomed to having more space.

In addition, Koreans have no code of behavior toward foreigners. The Confucian system does not demand respect or loyalty to people with whom one has no relationship. Only when a Korean forms a bond with a person does the latter stop being treated as a stranger, and the rules of respect and *kibun* come into play.

EDUCATION

As part of the Confucian heritage, education is highly valued by Koreans. Education was traditionally reserved for people of the highest class, the *yangban*. Today education is available to all Koreans. As a result of universal education, Korea boasts a 95 percent literacy rate.

In South Korea, there are five phases of education: one to two years in kindergarten, six in elementary school, three in middle school, three in high school, and four to six in college or university. North Korea has four levels: one year in kindergarten, four in elementary school, and six in middle school, followed by university.

After finishing middle, or high, school, students have several avenues to further their education. Besides the major universities, there are trade or industrial schools and evening classes in the south, and farming and industrial colleges in the north.

Education plays such an important role in the lives of Koreans that getting a good education is considered the key to a good career and a secure future. A South Korean teenager typically studies long hours in preparation for the annual university entrance examination that will determine his or her future. Students prepare years ahead for the eight-hour examination that tests their knowledge in mathematics, history, English, chemistry, literature, and physics. The examination is the sole factor in determining whether a student will be admitted to most universities. When students fail, they have to wait a full year before applying to another university and taking the examination again. If they fail the second time, there is no third chance.

There is intense competition for university places. Parents put a lot of effort into helping their children pass the examination. They hire tutors and change their lifestyle to offer moral and financial support in the months before the examination. In the past, sisters took factory jobs to bring in extra money so that their brothers could hire tutors. Mothers still wake up early in the morning to help their children begin studying. They also provide nourishing meals into the night. The pressure to excel academically is so great that some high-school students commit suicide because of poor scholastic results.

HOUSING

The traditional Korean home is an L-shaped, U-shaped, or rectangular single-story structure. Generally, the walls are built of clay and wood and the roof of thatch or tiles. But these typical houses can only be seen in rural parts of Korea today.

In cities, high-rise apartments abound to ease the housing shortage that has resulted from rapid urban growth since the Korean War. Newer buildings are made of concrete, and houses are

A family plays a traditional game sitting on their heated floor.

built to keep out cold air. Rooms are small, and doors and windows are few. Most houses have *ondol* (ON-doll), a heating system that dates back to the Stone Age. *Ondol* is a system of air pipes that are connected to the stove in the kitchen and pass under the floor. As the warm air from the stove passes through the pipes, it warms the floor, making it comfortable to walk or sit on.

Perhaps it is because of this heating method that most of the activities of a Korean family take place on the floor. Family members sleep and sit on mats on the floor. Even when dining, Koreans sit on the floor at low tables. Until recently there were few, if any, chairs or beds in a Korean home. Another practical custom that arose from having so much activity take place on the floor is that of always removing one's shoes before entering a home.

LIFE CYCLE

Koreans have unique rites and rituals to mark the milestones in their natural life cycle.

BIRTH The preference for male offspring is long-established in the patriarchal Confucian system. Korean wives have long faced a lot of pressure to bear a son to continue the family bloodline. The pressure has somewhat lessened, although the birth of a boy is still considered a greater blessing.

A *kumjul* is hung across the doorway of the house after the birth of a child.

Because it was so important to bear a son, wives offered prayers and followed rituals in the hope of having a baby boy. Offerings were made for 100 days to Taoist shrines, to the Buddha, and to various natural entities such as rocks and trees.

The main spirit concerned with childbirth is the *Samsin Halmeoni* (SUM-sin Hul-MO-neh), or grandmother spirit, who provides for the child even after it is born, guiding its growth and health. Her shrine is usually found inside the house and is represented by a piece of folded paper or clean straw hung in a corner.

For three weeks after birth, a straw rope of chili peppers or pine needles known as a *kumjul* (KEHM-jool) is hung across the doorway of the house to frighten evil spirits and warn people not to enter. Seaweed soup and rice are offered to the *Samsin Halmeoni* every morning and evening for a week. These foods are also eaten by the mother to speed up her recovery.

The newborn's family takes special care not to show their joy over the birth, because they believe the spirits may become jealous and cause the baby harm. To mislead the spirits, Korean babies are sometimes given unbecoming names.

A *dol* marks the child's survival during the crucial first year of life.

BIRTHDAYS Koreans celebrate their first and 60th birthdays, called *dol* (DOUL) and *hwangap* (HWUN-gup) respectively, in a grand way. A big party also takes place on a baby's 100th day of life, which in the past many failed to reach.

The 100th-day celebration, called *baegil* (PAY-gil), is quite a jubilee. It marks the baby's survival of a critical period that was once characterized by high mortality rates. Offerings of food are made to the *Samsin Halmeoni*, before family and friends celebrate with wine, rice cakes, and other delicacies. Finally, the guests present their gifts to the baby.

The *dol*, or first birthday, is celebrated in much the same way, but it is of even greater significance. Not only has the baby survived, but if it is a boy, he is ready to choose his future career.

The highlight of the event comes when the baby boy, dressed in the finest *hanbok*, is seated at a small table where his gifts and other items are placed. It is believed that the object that the child picks up from the table represents what he will become when he grows up. If it is a piece of string or yarn, he is supposed to live a long life. If it is money

BOY, WHERE ARE ALL THE GIRLS?

South Korea may face an unusual shortage, as the number of girls born steadily decreases. As recently as 1980, 108 boys were born for every 100 girls. By 1988 the proportion had risen to 113 boys for every 100 girls. The worldwide average is 102.5 boys per 100 girls, making Korea's proportion of males far greater than the global norm.

Have folk doctors in this male-dominated society found a way to conceive boys that Western doctors have not yet discovered? Experts think not but believe that medical technology is responsible for the growing gender-ratio imbalance.

Prenatal tests that reveal the gender of a fetus were introduced in South Korea in the early 1980s, just about the time the boy-girl birth ratio began to become distorted. Officials believe that pregnant women find out the gender of their child and abort the fetus if it is female.

In 1987 the practice of prenatal gender determination was outlawed in South Korea. By 1990 the penalty for doctors convicted of performing such tests was raised to a suspension of their medical license. The penalty was again made heavier in 1994 to possible imprisonment of up to a year, a fine of up to US$12,000, and revocation of the offender's medical license.

In the future, if the shortage of females becomes critical, parents will come to value daughters when their sons search in vain for a life partner.

"All Koreans go up one rank in prestige every year; they even start with a bonus— time in the womb counts as the first year of life, so that you are born at the age of one. Moreover, all birthdays occur on the Lunar New Year: if you are born in December, you are two almost before you can gurgle."

—*R.W. Howe, on Korean birthdays*

or rice, a business career awaits. If it is cake or other food, a career in government service is in the offing. If it is a musical instrument, he will become an artist. Guests leave the birthday party with packages of rice cakes given by the child's parents, who believe that sharing these rice cakes will bring the child good health and happiness.

The celebration of the 60th birthday, or *hwangap*, arose in the past when few people lived to that age. Also, the lunar calendar used by Koreans is based on 60-year cycles. Each year in the cycle has a different name, so when people reach their 60th year, the cycle returns to the year of their birth.

The family usually throws a lavish party, and loved ones gather to honor the celebrant. Rituals involve guests bowing to the celebrant and drinking wine, while traditional Korean music plays right through the party. Rice cakes and fresh fruit are served as part of the feast, and a photograph of the party group is taken to commemorate the event.

A ritual in a wedding ceremony.

MARRIAGE Few Koreans choose not to marry, since marriage is associated with maturity in Korea. In fact, an unmarried person is called a big baby in Korean slang. There are two kinds of marriages: love marriages, or *yonae* (yo-NAY); and arranged marriages, or *chungmae* (choong-MAY).

Chungmae are not as common in present-day Korea as they once were. The first step in an arranged marriage is for the two families to meet. The woman's parents probe the man's parents about his personality, his potential for success, and how he is likely to treat his wife. The man's parents set out to learn about the woman's character, health, and ability to fit into their family.

If the parents' meeting goes well, the young man and woman are left alone to get to know each other. They will not be forced to marry if they do not get along. But if they are compatible, they go out on a few dates and discuss their expectations of married life. When they are ready, they announce the marriage to their parents.

Regardless of whether a young Korean couple is entering into a love or arranged marriage, one or both of the mothers will probably visit a fortune-teller who will read the couple's astrological charts to check for compatibility and to determine an auspicious date for the wedding.

An engagement of two to three months is usual. In that time, both families must prepare gifts for one another.

THE TRADITIONAL WEDDING RITUAL

While most weddings in South Korea are Western-style ceremonies, some couples still marry traditionally. The bride's dowry depends on the prestige of the groom's family. The bride's family provides Western clothing for the groom's male relatives and Western clothing and traditional Korean dress for his female relatives. In addition, the bride often gives expensive jewelry to her future mother-in-law.

The groom sends the bride a *ham* (HAHM), a box of gifts—jewelry and fabric for a *hanbok*. A friend of the groom brings the box to the bride's home at a prearranged time and shouts that he has a *ham* for sale. The family must coax the box from him with wine and food.

The traditional wedding ceremony is held in the bride's home. It begins with an exchange of bows and drinks. The bride and groom face each other across a table with objects symbolizing their future together. The wedding ceremony is followed by another called the *pyebaek* (PAY-back), which is the bride's first greeting to her husband's family. It is at this time that the bride presents the groom's family with their gifts.

Afterward, the couple dresses in traditional Korean wedding clothes for official photographs and participates in bowing ceremonies to honor the marriage and the family.

The *chulssang,* or funeral procession, is a noisy affair that takes on the appearance of a festival.

OLD AGE Asians generally pride themselves on their care for the aged, and Koreans are no exception. With fewer extended families living in the same home, the way the elderly are cared for has changed. Nonetheless, the elderly in Korea are still treated with great respect, and children travel great distances each year to celebrate their parents' birthdays. Strangers will give up their seats for older people on buses and greet older people on the street with the appropriate honorific titles or language showing respect.

Old age is a time for leisure. Many older Koreans spend their free time traveling in tour groups around the country to visit famous attractions that they have heard about but never had a chance to see.

DEATH Korean customs and rituals surrounding death are also dictated by Confucian beliefs. Because of the emphasis on respect for parents and ancestors, careful attention is given to death rituals and funerals.

Dying at home is very important to Koreans. Doctors try to provide ample notice to a family when a relative is critically ill, so they can take the patient home before death. It is bad luck to bring a dead body home.

When someone dies, the body is covered with a white quilt, and formal wailing, or *kok* (kohk), announces the death. The body is arranged so that it faces south, in a ritual called *chohon* (CHOH-hon). The next step is *yom* (yohm), the preparation of the corpse, which entails bathing the body in perfumed water and dressing it in ritual burial clothes.

Notice of the death is sent out, and those who receive the notice visit the home of the deceased. This visit to pay respects to the deceased and offer condolences to the surviving family members is called *munsang* (MOON-sahng). Not conveying condolences is an offense to the grieving family and can create feuds and end friendships.

The *chulssang* (CHOOL-sahng) is the carrying of the coffin to the graveyard. This is accompanied by great fanfare, with some people carrying the coffin on their shoulders, some carrying flags and incense, and others ringing bells and singing mournfully.

At the burial ground, the family performs an ancestral ritual. Once the body is positioned to face south, the oldest son throws the first handful of dirt on the coffin.

Two old men enjoy an afternoon in the park. For Koreans, old age is the time to enjoy life.

RELIGION

THE SOUTH KOREAN CONSTITUTION guarantees its citizens freedom of worship. In North Korea, however, the communist regime does not encourage religious practice for fear it will weaken communist ideology. Shortly after the Korean War, the government closed down churches and temples or converted them for other purposes.

The majority of Koreans may say that they are Buddhist or Christian, but in reality they have mixed the beliefs and rituals of such religions with those of shamanism, an ancient form of spirit worship that is entrenched in the Korean way of life. For example, some Buddhist temples in Korea are carved with the figures of shamanist deities, and in the Korean version of the Christian bible, the word god is translated as *hanamin*, as the great spirit in shamanism is known.

SHAMANISM

Shamanism is a system of beliefs and practices that honor the spirits of nature. Korea's earliest form of religion does not aim for moral perfection. Shamanists believe that spirits inhabit everything, living and nonliving, and that spirits can pass between humans, plants, rocks, animals, and other objects.

Shamans, or *mudang* (MOO-dung), are usually women who act as intermediaries between people and spirits. They are believed to be able to influence spirits. *Mudang* are especially interested in the spirits of the dead and help resolve conflicts between the living and the dead. They perform ancient ceremonies to predict a brighter future for a customer, cure illnesses by exorcising evil spirits, and help guide spirits to heaven.

Above: **Spirit posts are erected to ward off evil spirits.**

Opposite: **The Tosonsa Buddhist Temple in Seoul.**

AT YOUR SERVICE: THE *KUT*

A shaman's treatment is sometimes little more than family therapy. The first step in solving almost any problem, be it a domestic quarrel or a financial situation, is to try to strengthen relationships among family members and household gods. If the problem worsens instead, the diagnosis is that the gods want to play or the family's ancestors are angry at certain family members. The solution is to hold a *kut* (KOOD), or shaman service.

The *kut* is a noisy ceremony, filled with shouting and the clanging of gongs. There is also singing, dancing, and chanting. The ceremony is a request to the gods or the ancestors to enjoy the festive atmosphere. This, it is believed, dispels all ill-will.

At some point in the service, the *mudang* lapses into a trance and acts as the receptacle of the spirits. She speaks to the gods or the ancestors, who speak back through her. As the service progresses, all the women of the household and even the neighbors present begin to participate by shouting to the supernatural visitors. Angry ancestors who cause illness can be exorcised by tossing grain, while angry gods can only be appeased with offerings and treats.

The *kut* may be held at the house of the person hiring the shaman, at the shaman's own home, or even outdoors, because the service must adapt to the type of problem it is addressing. The ceremony often goes on all night, and as day breaks, the shaman and her aides beat drums and perform a final exorcism for good luck.

BUDDHISM

Buddhism is one of the most popular religions in South Korea. Slightly less than 50 percent of the population are followers of Buddhism. Across the peninsula, there are thousands of Buddhist temples.

Buddhism began in Korea during the Three Kingdoms period. The religion is based on the teachings of the Buddha, Siddhartha Gautama, who was the prince of a small Indian kingdom in the sixth century B.C. The basic idea of Buddha's teachings is that salvation can come from giving up worldly desires and living in moderation. By living according to the Buddha's teachings, a Buddhist believes that he or she can reach the state of nirvana, ultimate peace, wherein a person experiences no pain or worry.

Worship at a Buddhist temple.

There are two main schools of Buddhism: Theravada and Mahayana. Korean Buddhism belongs to the Mahayana school, which is tolerant of local spiritual practices and puts no restriction on one's ability to reach salvation. Because Buddhism has been a part of the religious fabric of Korea for so many years, it has been mixed with some aspects of other religions, such as shamanism.

In fact, nearly every Buddhist temple in Korea has a chapel next to it that contains a shrine dedicated to the spirit of the mountain. The shrine receives the same respect that is bestowed on Buddhist shrines. This is done to avoid angering the local mountain spirit, upon whose land the Buddhist temple sits.

There are nearly 30,000 churches in South Korea. The country has about 2 million Catholics, and one in six South Koreans is Protestant.

TAOISM

Taoism came from China during the Three Kingdoms period, and the teachings of Lao Tzu, its founder, still persist in Korea today. Taoism found a ready following in Korea, as it is similar to shamanism in its worship of many equally important gods.

Taoism's main concern is to create harmony between humans and nature. The many gods are used as ideals toward which humans can strive. Taoists believe that spiritual perfection can be attained in this life through patience, purity, and peace.

Taoism never became overwhelmingly popular in Korea, but it influenced Korean society in numerous small ways. For example, the trigrams in the corners of the South Korean flag are derived from the *I-Ching*, the Chinese Book of Changes that Taoists use to divine the future.

CHRISTIANITY

Christianity was brought to Korea in the 16th century by Confucian intellectuals who learned about it in the Chinese capital, Peking (present-day Beijing). New converts to Christianity refused to participate in ancestral rites, and the government prohibited Christian missionaries from entering Korea.

The first half of the 19th century was a difficult time for Korean Christians. Thousands were persecuted, and many more were beheaded. Nonetheless, there were more than 20,000 Catholics in Korea by 1865.

THE UNIFICATION CHURCH

One of the most controversial religions in South Korea is the Holy Spirit Association for the Unification of World Christianity, or the Unification Church, founded in Korea in 1954 by Sun Myung Moon, a former Presbyterian minister.

After World War II, Moon began teaching principles that were considered contrary to Presbyterian beliefs. He was expelled from the Presbyterian Church in 1948. He started a new congregation, claiming to have had a vision of Jesus Christ giving him the mission of saving the world from Satan. These beliefs landed Moon in jail in North Korea. He escaped two years later and fled to South Korea, where he published his book, *The Divine Principle*. The book became the bible of the Unification Church.

The stated goal of the Unification Church is to establish the rule of God on earth, an effort that Moon's followers believe began with Jesus Christ but was interrupted by his crucifixion. Moon claims that Jesus Christ has entrusted him and his wife, Hak Ja Han, to complete the mission, and Moon's followers consider him to be the new messiah.

The Unification Church is said to have around three million members worldwide. Some members live on communes and do church-related work, usually fund-raising. Others are employed by one of the many business enterprises owned by the Unification Church, such as Pyonghwa Motors Company, a business venture in North Korea. In 2003 the Unification Church received permission from the South Korean government to organize tours to North Korea.

Today, with more than 22 million Christians, almost half its population, South Korea is second only to the Philippines in Asia in its percentage of Christians.

There are numerous denominations of Christianity, such as the Methodists and Presbyterians, in Korea. Most Protestant denominations in Korea are fundamentalist. Protestant fundamentalism emphasizes the literal interpretation of the bible as essential to Christian life.

A crowd entering an Evangelical church in South Korea.

There are also several minor Christian groups that some consider to be cult-like. A cult is generally described as a religious group devoted to a living leader or an unusual practice or teaching.

Dolharubang, statues carved from basalt, are thought to be ancient village guardian deities.

NEW RELIGIONS

South Korea officially categorizes more recent religious movements as new religions. There are nearly 250 new religions in South Korea. They generally combine indigenous beliefs with Christianity. Most of the new religions have small memberships.

The largest of South Korea's new religions is called Chondogyo, the Heavenly Way. It has a membership of approximately 600,000. The movement was founded in the 19th century by a scholar who claimed to have had a vision that called him to lead humankind in the ways of heaven. Chondogyo was originally called Tonghak, or eastern learning, to distinguish it from Catholicism, which spread from the West.

The communist government of North Korea views Chondogyo more warmly than it does other new religions. Chondogyo is similar to some aspects of communist ideology. The main Chondogyo belief is that all humans are equal and should be treated with respect because they have God within them.

WAITING FOR THE RAPTURE

Among the many new religions in South Korea, there is one that does not have much of a future, and its followers are thrilled. Members of the Mission for the Coming Days Church, about 20,000 of them, believe that the end of the world is coming and that a phenomenon called the Rapture will lift the faithful to heaven.

The only problem is that members of the movement do not seem to have a clear idea of when the world will end. The movement's officials warned members that October 28, 1992, would be the day when white-robed angels would carry them to heaven, trumpets announcing their arrival. The only remaining evidence of their previous existence on earth would be their clothing, dental fillings, and church identification tags.

According to officials of the doomsday movement, the Rapture would spark a seven-year war, resulting in flood, famine, and the eventual destruction of the planet. That, they said, would set the stage for Jesus Christ's second coming.

Believers made preparations, some going so far as to sell property, abandon family and military obligations, quit jobs, and even commit suicide. As the day approached, members spent up to 24 hours a day in one of the movement's 250 bases—basements, offices, and abandoned warehouses with leases that expired on October 28. They spent their time praying to be among the ones taken to heaven.

Nonuniform policemen monitored the movement's activity, but the government did not intervene, as the constitution guaranteed religious freedom. Eventually, other churches issued appeals to the government to quell the anxiety of the population.

When the day of the Rapture came and went without incident, the movement's members kept to their belief that their preparations would keep them in good faith for the next Rapture.

Another major new religion is Taejonggyo. It worships Dangun, the legendary founder of the Korean nation. That Taejonggyo is considered a new religion is ironic; it is actually Korea's oldest religion, dating back more than 4,000 years. It nearly disappeared in the 15th century, but in the last hundred years, several sects have arisen claiming to be a revival of the ancient faith. A few of the sects are very nationalistic, claiming that Korea will become a world empire and that a Korean will become the savior of humankind.

LANGUAGE

KOREA'S OFFICIAL LANGUAGE is also considered one of the world's major languages, because of the large number of people who speak it. Most language experts agree that Korean originated in central Asia in the Altai Mountains. It bears a resemblance to other languages in the Altaic family, such as Turkish, Finnish, Mongolian, and the Manchu-Tungus languages.

Korean is grammatically similar to Japanese, and half of its vocabulary is derived from Chinese. It has a logical writing system, *hangeul*, possibly the single most important thing that ever happened in Korea, because it brought literacy to the masses.

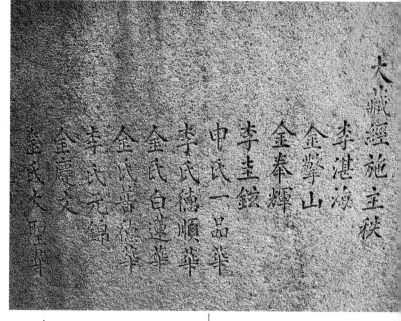

Above: **A rock carving of written Chinese, discovered in Busan. The Chinese writing system was used in Korea until the creation of *hangeul*, a phonetic system.**

Opposite: **Neon advertisements in Korean light up the night scene in Seoul.**

Regional Korean dialects are similar except for a few words that are pronounced slightly differently. South Korea's official dialect is the one used in the region of Seoul. Koreans living in different parts of the peninsula can usually communicate using their own dialects. The people of Jeju Island are the exception.

Korea's well-established social structure and its etiquette system call for different levels of language to appropriately distinguish between individuals and social classes. There are three language levels in use: a very polite form to address superiors; a personal form for speaking to equals or close friends; and a common or humble form for addressing people of a lower social level, or when referring to oneself.

Vowels Consonants	ㅏ [a]	ㅑ [ya]	ㅓ [ŏ]	ㅕ [yŏ]	ㅗ [o]	ㅛ [yo]	ㅜ [u]	ㅠ [yu]	ㅡ [ŭ]	ㅣ [i]
ㄱ [k,g]	가	갸	거	겨	고	교	구	규	그	기
ㄴ [n]	나	냐	너	녀	노	뇨	누	뉴	느	니
ㄷ [t,d]	다	댜	더	뎌	도	됴	두	듀	드	디
ㄹ [r,l]	라	랴	러	려	로	료	루	류	르	리
ㅁ [m]	마	먀	머	며	모	묘	무	뮤	므	미
ㅂ [p,b]	바	뱌	버	벼	보	뵤	부	뷰	브	비
ㅅ [s,sh]	사	샤	서	셔	소	쇼	수	슈	스	시
ㅇ [-]	아	야	어	여	오	요	우	유	으	이
ㅈ [ch,j]	자	쟈	저	져	조	죠	주	쥬	즈	지
ㅊ [ch']	차	챠	처	쳐	초	쵸	추	츄	츠	치
ㅋ [k']	카	캬	커	켜	코	쿄	쿠	큐	크	키
ㅌ [t']	타	탸	터	텨	토	툐	투	튜	트	티
ㅍ [p']	파	퍄	퍼	펴	포	표	푸	퓨	프	피
ㅎ [h]	하	햐	허	혀	호	효	후	휴	흐	히

The consonants and vowels of *hangeul*, the Korean alphabet.

HANGEUL

Sejong, the Joseon king from 1418 to 1450, was responsible for the development of *hangeul*. He wanted to enable all Korean people to write in their language. In his time, only the upper classes were educated and could decipher the Chinese characters representing the Joseon language.

Sejong faced great opposition to the project. Officials and scholars feared that Korean literature would be degraded—brought down to the level of dust—if it could be produced and understood by everyone. However, the king persisted, believing in literacy for all.

Hangeul was first known as *hunmin jeongeum*, or the right sounds for the instruction of the people. Sejong appointed scholars to devise a user-friendly alphabet system that closely represented the sounds of the Korean language as it was spoken then. The system was designed to be easy to read and write.

Hangeul uses a phonetic system of 24 characters: 14 consonants and 10 vowels. Each character represents a specific sound. Typically, two consonants sandwich a vowel between them to form a syllable. The 24 characters combine in many different ways to represent thousands of sounds and words in the Korean language.

Hangeul is easier to learn than many languages, including English. There are no capital letters, and vowels and consonants are easily differentiated. Handwritten *hangeul* may look like shorthand squiggles, but painted with a brush in calligraphy, *hangeul* looks like art.

VOCABULARY

As is the case with most modern languages, the Korean language consists of indigenous words and words borrowed from foreign languages. Many English words, such as aspirin, supermarket, and bus, have crept into the Korean language. Scientific and technological terms make up the majority of borrowed Western words.

Most borrowed words in Korean speech and writing come from the Chinese language, because Koreans have had contact with the Chinese for thousands of years. Chinese words assimilated into Korean are often called Sino-Korean words. Sino-Korean is to the Koreans what French is to the old aristocracies of Europe, a kind of elitist language.

Chinese numbers are generally used, especially after the number 10 and when counting items in successive order, such as in money and months.

STRUCTURE

In the Korean language, affixes add meaning to a root word or show its grammatical function. Verbs are generally the last element in a sentence, while the other parts can be switched around freely.

A Korean street sign.

Like Japanese, Korean has no articles (a, an, the), and singular and plural forms are usually the same. Also, the subject of a sentence is not mentioned when it seems apparent. For example, "Are you going?" and "Are they going?" would be asked in exactly the same way.

NAMES

Most Koreans have three names: the family name and two given names. The family name appears first. The first given name usually identifies one's generation and may be shared by siblings and cousins. The second given name may be a personality trait. Sons sometimes get one of their father's given names. For example, Kim Jong Il's second given name is the first given name of his father, the late North Korean president Kim Il Sung.

Koreans often consult shamans and sages before naming their babies. Choosing the right name is considered instrumental in bringing a person good fortune. Many Korean parents name their children after positive characteristics, such as wise or lovely, hoping that their children will grow up to personify their names.

Despite the fact that there are nearly 200 Korean surnames, half the population are Parks, Kims, and Lees. Some other relatively common family names in Korea are Shin, Han, Oh, Chang, and Choi.

Korean women do not change their family name when they marry. A woman may be addressed as Mrs. Min in conversation, since that is her husband's surname, but she is really known by her birth name throughout her life. She may also be called *ajumoni* (ah-JOO-moh-ni) or *puin* (POO-in), which both mean madam or aunty. Once she has a child, this form of address is replaced by one that indicates her new status. For example, if

A woman plays with her child. Koreans may call a married woman aunty, using the word in a very broad sense.

her oldest child is Sang-jun, she will be called Sang-jun's mother, even when he turns 50.

It is disrespectful to address the elderly by their given names. Generally, only family members and very close friends call a person by the given name.

TITLES

Titles are very important, because Koreans cannot communicate in the correct manner if they do not know the social status of the people they interact with. Titles are also necessary where many people share the same family name. For example, if several employees in a large company share the name Lee, the use of titles such as Director and Supervisor before the family name helps to avoid confusion. Titles may also reveal information about birthplace, schools, and so on, so that the proper measure of respect is shown when speaking to a superior.

HONORIFICS

Honorifics are polite forms of address reserved for older members of society or people of a higher social class. The most polite way to greet an older or more senior person in Korea is *ann-yong-ha-shim-ni-ga* (AHN-yong-HAH-shim-NI-kah).

A very polite form of address is always used when speaking to the elderly.

Honorifics also flatter. A Korean may address another as *Yangban*, an ancient title of nobility, just as a Westerner may address another as Boss. The title *Paksa* (PAK-sah), for teacher, may be used to address someone who has been offended, in the hope that he or she will assume the self-restraint expected of teachers and not be justly angry.

The *se-bae* (SAY-bay) is a special bow performed at weddings and other special occasions. The head is lowered all the way to the ground, and the palms touch the floor.

NONVERBAL COMMUNICATION

While certain behaviors, such as laughing or crying, are basic human reactions and convey the same emotive meaning all over the world, many nonverbal forms of communication are culture-bound and convey a specific meaning that only an understanding of the culture can interpret correctly.

BOWING Koreans bow when they meet and when they part. The person of lower status will bow first and say a greeting. Then the other person quickly bows and responds in kind. If the person being greeted is of much higher status (for example, a father receiving a greeting from his son), he may not bow, responding instead with an intimate greeting.

Bows range from a slight tilt to a right-angle bend to touching the ground. The greater the angle of the bow, the greater the respect shown. Someone who lowers his or her head all the way to the ground, palms touching the floor, shows the greatest degree of respect. This gesture is used in temples or homes, not in the office or on the street.

From the way two Koreans greet each other, an observer can easily distinguish the teacher, the doctor, and the grandfather from the student, the patient, and the grandson.

HAND GESTURES Korean hand gestures can be quite different from those used in the United States. For example, the wave that a North American understands as goodbye is the Korean signal to approach the waver. To wave goodbye, Koreans wave their raised forearm side to side, palm facing out. The American gesture for come, with the palm facing upward is used by Koreans only to call a dog. The way to call a person closer is to extend the arm with the palm downward, making a scratching motion.

Koreans use the right hand to pass an object to a superior. To show more respect, they use the left palm to support the right elbow. The greatest respect is shown by handing an object to a superior with both hands. Using the right hand is so associated with respect that children showing a tendency toward left-handedness are encouraged to rely more on their right hand.

It is impolite to maintain eye contact for a long time, so Koreans often look to either side during a conversation.

FACIAL EXPRESSION While Westerners try to maintain eye contact throughout a conversation, Koreans make eye contact only some of the time. When they are not looking into the eyes of the person they are conversing with, they will look to either side of the person's face, but not higher or lower.

People of higher status maintain eye contact longer than people of lower status do. Only in an argument or when transacting business do Koreans maintain constant eye contact. When being scolded, Koreans look down slightly. However, the eye-contact rule does not apply to strangers, and Koreans may stare at strangers if they are curious about them, a behavior some foreigners may find disconcerting.

Koreans smile when they are happy as well as when they are embarrassed or uncomfortable. A person who has displeased a superior may smile the whole day. When laughing, Korean women often cover their mouths.

ARTS

KOREAN ART has been largely influenced by Japan and China. While these countries share many characteristics in the arts, each has developed distinctive features. Korean arts usually revolve around such themes as love for nature, loyalty to the king, and admiration for learning. Korea's most developed art forms include sculpture, pottery, painting, music, dance, and poetry.

The dynasties that ruled Korea from A.D. 668 through the first few years of the 20th century encouraged the arts. Dancers and musicians were integral members of the court. But most of Korea's notable advancement in the arts came during the Unified Silla period (A.D. 668–917), when Buddhism had a profound effect on the arts and scholarship.

Countless temples, pagodas, and palaces were built, and paintings, ceramics, lacquerware, and jewelry flourished. Little is known of the artists, however. The works were often made by slaves ordered by the aristocracy, and slaves could not put their seal on their works.

From 1910 through the end of World War II, Japanese occupation impeded Korea's cultural pursuits. South Korea has made rapid and remarkable cultural advancement since 1948, focusing as much on traditional forms as on new innovations.

North Korea also strongly encourages the development of traditional fine arts. The government understands that such art forms provide a platform to promote nationalism. The nation's artists and writers are assigned to government institutions such as the national theaters and orchestras.

Above: **A performance of** *minsogak*, **music for the people.**

Opposite: **A mask maker carves expressive faces out of wood. The masks are worn by traditional mask dance performers.**

PANSORI

Korean narrative opera, known as *pansori* (PAHN-soh-ri), is an art form that captures the very character and culture of Korea by teaching traditional virtues through a story. An example of a *pansori* is the popular story of a young woman who withstands persecution to remain faithful to a noble admirer. The story touches on the important Korean qualities of loyalty, brotherly love, friendship, and respect for parents.

In *pansori*, a single performer beats out rhythms on a drum while vocalizing the roles and reciting the narrative between the songs. Although it is a one-man show, the performer appears to have a dialogue with the audience. A complete *pansori* can last up to six hours.

Korea's best-known *pansori* performer, Kim Myong Hwan, was in 1978 declared a living national treasure by the government.

While always considered a vital Korean art form, *pansori* has recently experienced a revival among students, some of whom have embraced it in rebellion against Western art forms. Other students draw on the techniques of this traditional drama format to satirize the contemporary political scene.

MUSIC

There are two kinds of traditional Korean music: *jeongak* (CHONG-gak) and *minsogak* (MIN-soh-gak). *Jeongak*, for the noble people, includes Confucian music, court music, and secular music of Chinese origin. *Minsogak*, for the common people, includes shaman music, Buddhist music, folk songs, *pansori*, and instrumentals, or *sanjo* (SAN-joh). Folk songs vary from region to region, but common to all are the shaman and Buddhist elements.

Music for farming dances is probably the oldest known Korean folk music, handed down from generation to generation since the Three Kingdoms period. The original purpose of this form of music was to appease the spirits of nature, but it later took on another function— entertainment—in addition to serving as a way to influence the spirits.

Nonetheless, some Koreans still believe folk music to have a positive effect on the spirits, and farmers still perform their traditional songs and dances to ensure a good harvest, purify the village's drinking water, or protect their homes.

Above: **Classical musicians play court music to an audience.**

Opposite: **Musicians sing and play the *gayageum* (KAH-yah-gehm), a 12-string zither.**

97

A Korean court dance.

DANCE

Traditional Korean dances have a close connection to agricultural cycles, having probably evolved from the shaman rituals that were performed more than 3,000 years ago to invoke the spirits.

Korean dances differ from most Western dances in at least one aspect: there is no choreography. Traditional Korean dances are supposed to be spontaneous and improvisational. A Korean dance does not tell a story as much as it conveys feelings. To do that, the dance involves two key concepts: *hung* (hahn) and *mot* (mot). *Hung* is a state of mind, an inner feeling or mood, while *mot* is grace and spiritual inspiration. To achieve *hung* and *mot*, the dancers have to rely more on their inner resources than on formulated dance techniques.

In traditional Korean dances, the arms and upper torso play a much greater role than the feet, which are often hidden under billowing skirts. Dance steps and poses are rare. Instead, there is a fluidity to the motion, which, combined with the airy costumes, gives the impression that the dancers are floating.

Korean dance can be broadly divided into two kinds: court and folk. Court dances are performed by both men and *kisaeng*, or female entertainers. Court dances were once performed solely for a royal audience. The elaborate costumes contrast with the simple steps.

There are two types of court dance, one of Korean origin and the other of Chinese origin. The most popular court dance is called *Hwaganmu* (HWA-kwan-moo), or Flower Crown Dance, named after the dancers' flowered crowns.

Folk dances are the most representative of Korean dances and can be divided into religious dances, which are led by monks, and secular dances, which are performed by ordinary people. Farming dances, in which dancers spin wildly to the beat of drums and gongs, are the oldest surviving dances in Korea. Folk dances continue to be performed to welcome good spirits and drive away evil.

Mask dances originated during the Joseon era (1392–1910). The quality of a mask dance lies in the skill of the actor. The more lively the actor, the more animated the dance.

The best-known of the religious dances are the shaman dances that invoke the spirits to send the *mudang,* or shaman, into a trance. Others in the religious category are Confucian dances—stiff, ceremonial forms that were first performed in China. Confucian dances are performed at shrines in Korea during ceremonies in spring and winter.

Perhaps the most distinctive of all Korean folk dances are the mask dances. They were originally a means for people to express anger and disappointment toward the government and clergy. The themes of mask dances include corruption, greed, hypocrisy, stupidity, and fraud. The masks are the focus of the satirical dramas. Drums, cymbals, and flutes provide the musical accompaniment. The masks are burned after each performance, because it is thought that the spirits contaminate them.

LITERATURE

Classical Korean literature focuses almost exclusively on history and nature. Before the 20th century, almost all Korean literature was written in Chinese, because many scholars despised *hangeul*, the alphabet that was created for all Koreans.

Korea's best-known literary works are treasured not only for their literary worth but also for the historical information they contain on ancient Korea. *History of the Three Kingdoms* was written in the 12th century, and *Memorabilia of the Three Kingdoms* in the 13th century.

Korean poetry dates back to the sixth century. Six- to 12-line lyrical poems called *hyangga* (HYUNG-gah) were written during the Silla dynasty using Chinese characters. After the advent of *hangeul*, a poetic form known as *sijo* became popular. *Sijo* is a very short ode, sometimes only three lines long. As people became more proficient in writing *hangeul*, they found that the short *sijo* could not convey their complex emotions, so they began using a longer poetic form called *kasa* (KAH-sah). Familiar to all Koreans, *sijo* and *kasa* are two of the most characteristic forms of Korean poetry.

Korean novels also appeared after *hangeul* entered the picture. Two of the most famous early Korean novels are *Tale of Lady Sa* and *Dream of the Nine Clouds*. Many of Korea's early novels were also written about military experiences. The period from 1725 through 1800 is considered the time when traditional Korean fiction really came of age.

A SIJO

This verse was composed by Hwang Chi-ni, a famous *kisaeng* from the Three Kingdoms period who wrote *sijo*. *Kisaeng* were women who entertained men with music and dance.

Alas, what have I done?
    Didn't I know how I would yearn?
Had I but bid him stay,
    how could he have gone? But stubborn
I sent him away,
    and now such longing learn!

—*Translated by David R. McCann*

Korean literature from the 20th century onward has focused on social and political issues. The historical novel remains popular among both readers and writers.

PAINTING

The early Korean painters were influenced by the Chinese. Chinese-style Korean wall paintings dating back to A.D. 400 have been found in tombs in Goguryeo (present-day North Korea). The bright-colored paintings depict the peoples and lifestyles of Korea around the time of Christ. Some paintings had Chinese mythical figures, such as the sun, the moon, and dragons. Korean painting developed its own natural form during the Joseon dynasty. Distinctive styles of composition and treatment of space emerged, as did brush-stroke techniques.

Women are taught the basics of Korean painting. The paintings in the background focus on nature scenes.

Korean folk painting was overlooked for centuries, because it was produced by the less educated classes. Confucian scholars spurned the colorful works of the common people, because they did not reflect the "correct" religious and intellectual values. It was customary to destroy or bury old paintings whenever new ones were created, so many old folk paintings were lost forever.

Minhwa (MIN-hoo-wa), Korea's folk paintings, give a real view of everyday life. The main theme of *minhwa* is the relationship between people and their environment—a theme that is expressed in Buddhism, Taoism, shamanism, and Confucianism. *Minhwa* is seen as a true indigenous artistic expression of the Korean people.

CALLIGRAPHY

Calligraphy is an art form more highly regarded than painting in Korea, China, and Japan. Throughout history, calligraphy has had a strong influence on Korean culture. It is taught in schools by masters of calligraphy.

Calligraphy is the composition of a few characters in an aesthetically pleasing manner. Although *hangeul*, the Korean writing system, was invented in the mid-1400s, Chinese was used as the official script until the late 1800s.

As Confucianism and its focus on the importance of education developed during the Joseon period, calligraphy became a cherished skill. Among the nobility, the only class that knew how to write, calligraphy was considered an essential discipline for a refined gentleman.

Truly artistic calligraphy depends on the creativity and talent of the writer, who can render interesting shapes to the strokes of the written characters. Each stroke must be perfect—there is no retouching or shading—and balanced, which requires skill that can only come with years of practice. Communication is not the main thrust of calligraphic writing. Rather, it is admired in its totality as a well-executed piece of art. This exquisite, stylized writing is considered an art form closely related to painting and is hung on walls as paintings are displayed.

SCULPTURE

Archeological diggings have revealed clay, bone, and stone figures of animals and man from Neolithic times, but it is believed that sculpture really began to develop after Buddhism was introduced to the Korean peninsula, around A.D. 500. A classic piece of sculpture from this period is a gilt-bronze standing image of Buddha that was discovered in 1967. An inscription on it corresponds to the year A.D. 537.

Some of the most remarkable accomplishments in stone art sculpture are found in the Seokguram Grotto Shrine, dating to A.D. 900. The shrine has 37 stone images considered to be among the most beautiful Korean sculptures.

Pagodas and stupas, which are cylindrical Buddhist shrine mounds, are also considered typical of Korean sculptural art. Most are decorated with Buddhist images and religious designs.

Modern sculpture in Korea began to gain popularity in the 1960s. Realism and abstract ideas were more greatly appreciated, and an increasing number of materials were used. Two major movements emerged. One, known as the "anti-formal abstract movement," became quite popular, as sculptors freely expressed their emotions through unconventional, abstract shapes. Then the "sculptural conceptualism movement" evolved, producing simple forms. Current sculptural trends are taking on a more nostalgic, humane nature.

CRAFTS

METALCRAFT A great number of relics of ancient ages have been uncovered in Korea. Relics of the Bronze Age, including mirrors, knives, bells, belt hooks, and ornamental ritual ware have been found all over the peninsula. Metalcraft was a refined art in Korea by 100 B.C. One of the truly exceptional Korean metalcraft products is bells. Only a few, dating back to the Silla dynasty (A.D. 668–917), remain today, and their artistic merit has been acknowledged throughout the world.

POTTERY Perhaps the best-known of Korea's art objects is pottery. Almost every museum in the Western world has some Korean celadon pottery. Celadon was first produced in Korea in about A.D. 1050, when artisans discovered a way to inlay design on pottery, which was glazed and fired at an extremely high temperature. The method produced pieces in a watery blue-green color that are now famous. Celadon pottery has a range of different colors.

The 1,000-year-old Emillie Bell is a perfect model of the ancient Korean art of bronze bell sculpture. It is Korea's largest bell, 10 feet (3 m) high and weighing 20 tons (20,000 kg).

LEISURE

THE KOREAN WORK WEEK is one of the world's longest, leaving little leisure time. But Koreans bring the same intense attitude they apply at work to sports, television, and the nightlife. North Koreans have a more austere lifestyle than South Koreans, with regimented leisure activities such as organized museum tours, but they too enjoy vigorous games.

Hostility between north and south has occasionally tarnished sportsmanship. There have been unfortunate events, such as North Korea's boycott of the 1988 Seoul Olympics. Yet, in 1991 the two nations sent combined table-tennis teams to Japan and emerged champions, a good omen to Koreans hopeful for reunification.

Above: **Young North Koreans take a break from their military duties to enjoy a volleyball game.**

Opposite: **Korean children playing in a palace garden in Seoul.**

SPORTS

The popularity of sports in Korea has increased steadily. Koreans are health-conscious and highly competitive. They consider athletic activity essential to physical development and involve their children in sports —friendly or competitive—very early in life.

SOCCER International sports have slowly made their way into Korea. Soccer, the most popular, was brought to Korea in 1882 by sailors on a merchant ship. South Korea's soccer team is a premier player in Asia. At the 1986 Asian Games, South Korea won gold in soccer, and at the 2002 FIFA World Cup, South Korea came in fourth, becoming the first Asian soccer team to reach the world semi-finals.

WORLD-CLASS SPORTING ACHIEVEMENTS

Korean sportsmen and sportswomen have made a name for their country internationally. More importantly, their admirable achievements are helping to bond the two Koreas in the hope that their nations will one day cease to compete against each other and start playing together as one united team at international competitions.

TABLE TENNIS The first ever attempt by North and South Korea to unite in the sporting arena took place in 1991. It was a major breakthrough since North Korea prevented South Korea from competing in the 1979 world championship in Pyongyang by not issuing the Seoul team visas. In 1991 the two Koreas sent a joint team to the world championship held in Japan. They won.

Before that historic event, at the Asian Games in Seoul in 1986, South Korea beat long-time champion China in three table-tennis events.

ARCHERY South Korean archers are keen competitors at the Asian and Olympic games. They swept all top three medals in the women's category at the 2000 summer Olympics and took the gold in both the men's and women's events at the world archery championship in 2003.

GOLF South Korea's top woman golfer, Pak Se Ri, is a high-ranking LPGA (Ladies Professional Golf Association) player, having won numerous tournaments and emerged runner-up in the U.S. Women's Open. Grace Park is another dominating force on the world women's circuit, while up-and-coming 13-year-old Michelle Wie is the longest-hitting woman golfer. In men's golf, South Korea's Choi Kyung Ju has two U.S. PGA tour titles.

SOCCER At the 2002 FIFA World Cup, South Korea was more than co-host. The nation became a force in the international soccer scene, advancing steadily through each match. While South Korea eventually lost to Germany in the semi-finals, that they got so far was enough reason to celebrate. South Korea made history by becoming the only Asian soccer team to reach the World Cup semi-finals. Coach Guus Hiddink gained an almost god-like status in South Korea and was made an honorary citizen of Seoul by the city's mayor.

BASEBALL Baseball came to Korea in 1905 with Christian missionaries from the United States. Today, national baseball tournaments are major events that draw large crowds in South Korea. A baseball league was established in the 1980s, and in 1984 South Korea showed its ability to compete internationally when it won the World Little League title.

Major-league clubs include the Tigers, the Lions, and the Unicorns, sponsored by large corporations such as Kia Motors, Samsung, and

Hyundai. The clubs are members of the Korean Baseball Organization, which markets the teams and organizes annual competitions.

VOLLEYBALL Another 20th-century import to Korea is volleyball. It is played by men and women, recreationally and professionally. Korean men's and women's volleyball teams compete in the Asian Games and internationally. Koreans are also recruited to coach volleyball teams in other countries.

ARCHERY Archery is one of Korea's oldest sports, one in which women could participate without fear of criticism. Today, Korean students and working adults can join clubs registered with the Korea Traditional Archery Association. Members take part in competitions that rank them according to the number of hits they make.

OTHER SPORTS Other sports that are played and enjoyed in Korea include golf, boxing, tennis, table tennis, rifle-shooting, and skiing.

Korean women gear up for a shot at an archery competition.

TAE KWON DO A self-defense martial art that originated in Korea more than 2,000 years ago, tae kwon do is considered Korea's national sport. Nearly every Korean man will take up the sport at some point in his life. Tae kwon do has become popular around the world. Korean tae kwon do instructors train people in many countries.

WRESTLING *Ssireum* (SEE-rehm), meaning the competition of man, is a Korean form of wrestling similar to Japanese sumo wrestling. *Ssireum* is believed to have originated as a means of self-defense more than 1,500 years ago. Over time, it became a sport. *Ssireum* has simple rules. Each contestant twists and turns, pushes and pulls, until one manages to force a part of the other's body to touch the ground. *Ssireum* is a favorite physical activity among fishermen and farmers. It is also taught in Korean middle and high schools.

A *tae kwon do* demonstration.

TRADITIONAL GAMES

Traditional Korean games developed over centuries. Many of them have their roots in China, and few are truly Korean. Because Korea was such a poor nation for so many years, many of their traditional games require very little equipment. They are customarily played during festivals.

TOP SPINNING *Paengi-chigi* (PAIN-gee-JIG-gee), or top spinning, is a popular pastime among Korean children. They hold sticks with strings

attached and whip the sharp base of their wooden tops to keep them spinning. In winter, children also play *paengi-chigi* on ice.

Two *chajon-nori* competitors pit their strength against each other at a festival.

DAK SSAUUM *Dak ssaum* (DUCK-saom) is a slightly more physically challenging game for children, and it does not require any equipment. Players have to hold one foot up behind them with their hands and try to knock down their opponents while hopping around.

BADUK *Baduk* (BAH-dook) is a game of strategy, a battle of wits, for adults. The *baduk* board is a grid pattern formed by 19 vertical and 19 horizontal lines. One player uses black stones and the other white to try to conquer and guard squares and capture each other's stones. Most Koreans know how to play *baduk* at least recreationally, and *baduk* professionals compete in international tournaments.

CHAJON-NORI *Chajon-nori* (CHAH-john-NOH-ri) is a two-man battle on poles. Two sets of poles are raised at an angle from the ground so that they meet at the top. Near the top of each set of poles, a man supports himself using rope and tries to knock his opponent down, while his teammates on the ground hold the poles up to steer him to victory.

Korean women playing neolttwigi.

KOREAN CHESS Like Western chess, *janggi* (CHANG-gi) symbolically represents war, and each player has 16 pieces to maneuver. The object is to capture the general. A young or amateur player is always allowed to make the first move in *janggi*.

SEESAW Mostly women enjoy *neolttwigi* (NOL-di-gi). A long plank is pivoted in the center on a bag of rice straw or a rolled-up straw mat. A woman stands on one end of the plank, another on the other end. One jumps as hard as she can, and when she lands on her end of the plank, her friend on the other end bounces up high in the air. *Neolttwigi* was traditionally a way for Korean women to catch glimpses of the world outside the high fence around their yard.

KITE-FLYING Flying kites, or *yeon* (YAWN), is a popular recreational activity for both young and old in Korea. The kites are almost always rectangular, with a round hole in the center. They are made from paper and bamboo, held together with glue, and decorated with geometric

designs. The Lunar New Year is kite-flying season, and on the last day of the new moon, people traditionally let their kites go, hoping that bad luck will float away with them.

Yunnori is usually played on Lunar New Year's Day. A lot of the fun comes from the cheering of those watching.

YUNNORI Originally a game to divine future events, *yunnori* (YOON-nori) is believed to have been brought to Korea by the Mongols. Players throw four sticks in the air. The sticks are flat on one side and curved on the other. Points are given according to which side touches the ground when the sticks land, and the team with the most points in each turn advances around a circle. The first team to finish wins.

TUG-OF-WAR Two teams each make a straw rope of an agreed length and thickness. The ropes are then knotted together, and the tug begins. The team pulling on one end represents the female side, while the team on the other end represents the male side. Traditionally, entire villages competed in tug-of-war games, and when the female side won, it was believed to symbolize a good harvest.

111

FESTIVALS

KOREANS CELEBRATE two kinds of festivals. Generally, the older, more traditional festivals have a cultural or religious background, while the newer, more modern festivals arose out of political events in the two nations' histories.

Most North Korean holidays are political anniversaries, such as its leaders' birthdays and its Constitution Day, while many South Korean festivals are agriculturally based, since the people of the peninsula were an agricultural society for centuries.

Both countries celebrate a few imported festivals as well as many homegrown ones. In addition, with increasing Westernization, Koreans have mixed their styles of celebration, incorporating certain aspects of modern urban lifestyles, such as fashion and food, into the celebration of some traditional festivals.

Left: **The drum accompanies Korean festivals.**

Opposite: **Koreans walk under a canopy of lanterns at a temple in Seoul during the festivities of the Buddha's birthday.**

Children offer a formal bow to their elders on Lunar New Year's Day.

NEW YEAR'S DAY

New Year's Day occurs twice a year in Korea. January 1 is a national holiday in North and South Korea, when Koreans celebrate with the rest of the world. Koreans also observe the Lunar New Year. South Koreans enjoy three days off work during the Lunar New Year, or Seollal.

Younger Koreans generally consider January 1 the start of the new year. Their elders, however, put greater emphasis on lunar dates and mark the start of the new year on the lunar calendar.

A lot of preparation precedes the Lunar New Year. Homes are cleaned and debts repaid. The focus of the festival is the honoring of one's elders and ancestors. Children wear new *hanbok* and socks and shoes to bow and offer their respects to their parents and grandparents, who in turn give them their blessings and money or other small gifts. People send one another greeting cards and exchange simple handmade gifts during the Lunar New Year.

Family gatherings and visiting friends are also important activities during the Lunar New Year. Cousins, aunts, uncles, and other relatives come together at the home of the eldest member of the extended family for a memorial service to their dead ancestors, a tradition originating in Buddhism. Food is prepared and set in front of photographs of the deceased. Everyone bows to the photographs, and then the younger people bow to their eldest living relatives.

Over the next few days, Koreans visit other people to whom respect is due. For example, employees visit their bosses, students visit their teachers, and so on.

THE FIRST FULL MOON

Dae-bo-rum, or the first full moon, is celebrated on the 15th day of the first lunar month. In the past, the Korean New Year festivities ended on Dae-bo-rum.

Koreans have always been fascinated by the moon. Farmers used to think they could predict the weather for the coming months by the color of the first full moon. A golden moon foretold perfect weather, and a reddish moon meant little rain.

During Dae-bo-rum, fire signals the momentous sighting of the first full moon in the lunar year.

Koreans traditionally believe that catching a glimpse of the first full moon rising brings good luck for the coming year. People gather in the afternoon, often on a hilltop, to wait to see the rim of the rising moon. Those in the countryside light little mounds of twigs to signal the momentous event.

The first full moon is a very cheerful and rousing time in Korea. Neighboring villages engage in tug-of-war competitions and mock torch fights and stone fights. Youths spend the day searching for good-luck charms and doing things nine times for good luck.

Special Dae-bo-rum foods include peanuts, chestnuts, and walnuts. It is thought that such foods will keep one's skin clear the whole year. A dish called *o-gok-pap* (OH-gohk-pahp), made of five grains, is a traditional offering during this festival.

Pink-flowering cherry trees mark the beginning of spring.

CHERRY BLOSSOM FESTIVAL

When spring begins in Korea in early April, the cherry trees bloom, and their pretty pink flowers fill the air with a sweet scent. So lovely are the cherry trees in spring that people go out for the whole day just to enjoy the beauty of the cherry blossom festival.

The Japanese planted Korea's first cherry trees in Jinhae, where they had their naval headquarters during the colonial period (1910–45). At the end of World War II, when the Japanese surrendered and the South Koreans gained independence, most of the cherry trees in Korea were uprooted, because they reminded the Koreans of the Japanese.

New cherry trees have since been planted in Jinhae, and the cherry blossom festival continues to be enjoyed but with a different focus. Koreans now celebrate the festival in honor of the famed Admiral Yi Sunsin, who in the 16th century defeated Japanese soldiers in the Imjin War. Parades, concerts, and traditional games are held to celebrate his victory every spring.

THE BUDDHA'S BIRTHDAY

The Buddha's birthday is celebrated on the eighth day of the fourth lunar month, which is sometime between late April and late May. On that day, Buddhists attend some of the numerous religious ceremonies and events held at temples throughout the country.

Once the state religion of the Korean peninsula, Buddhism fell from favor during the Joseon dynasty. It was then that Confucianism replaced it as a social force. In spite of that, Buddhism still ranks as one of the religions of Korea.

On the Buddha's birthday, colorful paper lanterns and flowers adorn the courtyards of temples, and tags printed with the names of people's ancestors hang from the lanterns. Koreans congregate at the temples to offer their prayers and ask for the Buddha's blessing. Many bring home-made lanterns. Others bring flowers to the altar of the Buddha or burn incense before the altar. The day culminates with an evening parade of candlelit lanterns. The light symbolizes hope.

Devout Buddhists offer prayers on the Buddha's birthday.

117

A band at a Children's Day celebration.

CHILDREN'S DAY

South Koreans celebrate Children's Day on May 5, and North Koreans on June 6. The holiday originated during the Japanese occupation of Korea. It replaced what was previously Boys' Day, reflecting a social consciousness that all children, not just boys, should be treasured.

On Children's Day, Korean children receive gifts from their parents. They often wear their traditional dress when visiting the many public pageants and martial-arts demonstrations held in their honor.

DANO DAY

Koreans have celebrated Dano Day, also known as Swing Day, for centuries. The holiday falls on the fifth day of the fifth lunar month—generally sometime between late May and late June.

This festival originated as a day to pray for good harvests and is especially important among people living in rural areas. According to

Koreans go all out to celebrate Dano Day.

ancient records, farming activity stopped on Dano Day, and there were festivities similar to those of the Lunar New Year.

Dano Day is usually celebrated out of doors. People in villages assemble in the village square, marketplace, or other common space, while people in cities gather in parks and other open-air event venues to watch and take part in the day's festivities. There are puppet shows, wrestling matches, swinging contests, and a whole lot of dancing. Many of the events have their origin in the ancient celebration of the Dano festival when it was not often that women were allowed to leave the confines of their homes and celebrate in the presence of men.

Men display their strength in wrestling, or *ssireum*, matches, and the winner gets a bull as a prize. Women take part in swinging contests. The villages usually set up a long swing on the branch of an old tree, and the women of the town compete to see who can swing the highest standing up. The winner sometimes gets a gold ring. Mask dances are performed in some regions to drive away evil spirits.

A procession to grave sites on Chuseok.

THE HARVEST MOON

Chuseok, the harvest moon, is celebrated on the 15th day of the eighth lunar month, when the moon is brightest, sometime between early September and early October. Families return to their ancestral homes to attend memorial ceremonies in honor of their ancestors.

The Chuseok family feast includes a traditional rice cake filled with bean paste or honey-sweetened sesame seeds. After the feast, some Koreans dress in traditional clothing and visit graves to make food offerings and bow to their ancestors.

Koreans have long believed that the moon inspires creativity. In the early days, the harvest moon festivities usually ended with the viewing of the full moon and poetry reading and writing.

CHRISTMAS

Christmas is not a major holiday in Korea, although there is a growing Christian population in South Korea. People attend Christmas church services during the season and reflect on the significance of the birth of Jesus Christ and thank God for the gift of His son.

Commercially, Christmas in Korea is similar to Christmas in the West. People decorate their homes, sing carols, shop for gifts in stores with elaborate displays, and enjoy festive feasts.

KOREA'S CALENDAR OF OFFICIAL HOLIDAYS

Many of South Korea's festivals are derived from the agricultural cycle. For centuries, farmers planted and harvested on special days, which were marked on the lunar calendar based on the phases and positions of the moon. These festivals continue to be celebrated today, but not all of them can be declared public holidays. A list of South Korea's official holidays follows:

January 1	New Year's Day
January/February	Lunar New Year (Seollal)
March 1	Independence Movement Day
April/May	Buddha's birthday
April 5	Arbor Day, an imported tree-planting festival that is also observed in Canada, Israel, the United States, and parts of Europe.
May 5	Children's Day
June 6	Memorial Day, a day of tribute to the war dead
July 17	Constitution Day
August 15	Liberation Day, the anniversary of liberation from Japan in 1945
September/October	Chuseok (Thanksgiving)
October 3	National Foundation Day, or Dangun Day, the traditional founding of Korea by Dangun in 2333 B.C.
December 25	Christmas Day

Most of North Korea's holidays celebrate the anniversaries of political events in its history or the birthdays of its leaders. Such holidays have been observed for only a few decades. A list of North Korea's official holidays follows:

January 1–2	New Year's Day
January/February	Lunar New Year
February 16–17	Birthday of Kim Jong Il
March	Hansik, the cleaning and weeding of ancestral graves
April 15–16	Birthday of the late Kim Il Sung
April/May	Dano Day
May 1	May Day
August 15	Liberation Day, the anniversary of liberation from Japan in 1945
September/October	Chuseok (Thanksgiving)
September 9	Foundation Day
October 10	Launch of Workers' Party
December 27	Constitution Day

FOOD

A PARTICULARLY POPULAR Korean greeting in the countryside is *"PAM-MO-GO-SSO-YO* (PAHM-moh-goh-soh-yoh)?" It translates as "Have you had rice today?" Rice is a staple of the Korean diet. The greeting implies that you are fine if you have had rice, and if you have not had rice, then you should have some.

Koreans eat three meals a day. Food that is eaten for breakfast, lunch, and dinner are similar. The difference is the number of side dishes, or *banchan* (bun-CHAHN). As many as six side dishes are served for breakfast, a dozen for lunch, and nearly 20 for dinner.

Each meal generally includes rice, a traditional Korean pickle called *kimchi* (KIM-chee), and soup, which doubles as a drink. Koreans do not usually have tea with their meal. The soup contains several ingredients, such as beef, tofu, mung beans, and vegetables. There are special soups for special occasions, such as weddings, births, and New Year celebrations. Red pepper, green onion, garlic, sesame oil, and soy sauce give Korean food a strong aroma and make it easily identifiable among other Asian cuisines.

Above: **A street vendor waits for customers before serving hot, freshly cooked meals.**

Opposite: **Korean pancakes are made with seafood or vegetables.**

KIMCHI

Opposite, top: Gimjang, or kimchi-making season, is a time when Koreans chop, season, and mix loads of kimchi in a mini-assembly plant at home.

Opposite, bottom: Kimchi earthenware pots stored in the yard.

Kimchi is Korea's signature dish of spicy, pickled vegetables. Said to be high in vitamins and nutrients, the fermented delicacy is eaten at every meal with rice. *Kimchi* is closely associated with the national identity.

Kimchi ferments without vinegar, and the predominant flavor is red pepper. Culinary experts consider *kimchi* the king of pickles. There are probably more than 200 varieties of *kimchi*, but mainly two varieties are eaten in all Korean homes: whole cabbage and hard radish. The whole cabbage variety consists of salted cabbage, sliced vegetables, herbs and spices, fermented fish sauce, fresh oysters, garlic, and chilies. The hard radish variety consists of cubed radish, sliced cabbage, and a few other kinds of vegetables.

In summer, *kimchi* is prepared weekly, since the vegetables are in season. But when winter sets in, no crops can be produced until late spring. The approach of winter marks the start of a long *kimchi*-making time called *gimjang* (KIM-jahng). Before November ends, when the weather has cooled and the crops are in from the fields, the outdoor markets are burgeoning. Koreans start slicing and spicing, preparing enough *kimchi* to last through winter.

During *gimjang*, Koreans gather in groups to cut, wash, and salt hundreds of pounds of cabbage and white radish. After it is prepared, *kimchi* is stored in the yard in large earthenware crocks. In the countryside, the crocks are buried up to their necks to keep the pickled vegetables from freezing.

While refrigerators are now widely available in Korea, many people still follow the *gimjang* tradition that has been passed down to them from older generations. Even Koreans living in the big cities store crocks of *kimchi* on the balcony of their apartment.

Seoul is home to the world's only Kimchi Museum. The museum aims to preserve the art and culture of making *kimchi*, in a nation where people living busy city lives find it more convenient to buy mass-produced *kimchi* off shop shelves than make their own at home. The Kimchi Museum gives Koreans and tourists alike a chance to taste different varieties of *kimchi* and to learn how to make traditional *kimchi*.

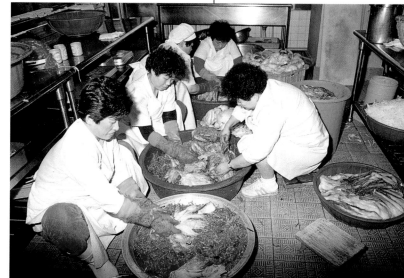

CHOPSTICKS

To Koreans, picking up bite-size bits of food using a pair of sticks is second nature. But to people who are used to eating with their fingers or with knife and fork, using chopsticks can get them in a tangle.

The trick to using chopsticks is to hold the chopstick that is closest to the palm still, while moving the other chop -stick back and forth. One chopstick thus acts as a pivot for the other so that both work together like pincers to hold pieces of food.

The first chopstick is tucked under the base of the thumb, with the lower

part lightly resting on the inside of the ring finger. The second chopstick is held like a pencil between thumb and forefinger. The tips are then brought together around a piece of food and moved to the person's mouth. It takes some practice before the motions are perfected.

TABLE MANNERS

In a traditional Korean home, the men of the house are served first, and the women must wait until they are no longer needed to replenish the plates, bowls, and cups. Only after the men finish do the children and women eat. Sometimes the women and children eat in the kitchen, while the men eat in the living room. In modern Korean households, the whole family eats together.

Each diner is equipped with a pair of chopsticks and a soup spoon. Once the meal begins, the chopsticks never touch the table. Neither are they ever stuck straight up in the rice. Instead, the diner rests his or her chopsticks across the rice bowl.

No one at the table starts eating until the eldest person takes the first bite. Rice is served in individual bowls, and each person is expected to finish his or her serving. The side dishes are shared by everyone. There is little or no talking during meals. To show one's satisfaction, slurping

BULGOGI

Bulgogi, thin strips of spicy grilled beef, is probably Korea's best-known dish next to *kimchi*. This recipe makes 12 servings.

4 tablespoons soy sauce	4 tablespoons toasted sesame seeds
2 tablespoons sesame oil	1½ pounds (¾ kg) sirloin tip, thinly sliced
2 tablespoons sugar	12 leaves romaine lettuce
½ teaspoon black pepper	1 cup cooked rice
1 clove garlic, finely chopped	ground cayenne pepper

In a large bowl, combine the soy sauce, sesame oil, sugar, black pepper, garlic, and sesame seeds. Add the meat strips, and stir. Cover and refrigerate for 2 hours, then cook on a barbecue grill or in a preheated oven for 2 to 3 minutes on each side. Place a serving of the cooked meat strips on a lettuce leaf with 2 teaspoons of hot rice. Add a dash of cayenne pepper, then roll up the leaf, and serve hot.

soup or noodles is customary, while older Koreans burp at the end of the meal.

In formal settings, Koreans eat rice not with chopsticks but with a spoon. They also avoid holding food with their fingers or making noises such as slurping and burping.

TYPICAL MEALS

While the three daily meals in Korea differ in the number of side dishes, they all share in common rice, *kimchi*, and soup, and a seasonal fruit closes the meal.

Contrast and color are important in Korean meals. Plain rice goes with spicy side dishes, and cold salads go with hot soups. The colors of the ingredients make the meal look appetizing.

Traditionally, Korean food is served in small bowls that are neatly arranged on a low table. Some restaurants in South Korea set the tray in the kitchen before carrying it out to the diners.

A typical Korean dining-table setup.

127

ENTERTAINING GUESTS

Koreans spare no expense in entertaining guests in their homes. They consider it a matter of great pride to make the home comfortable and to prepare a special meal that is pleasing to their guests.

The meal is usually preceded by drinks served in the living room. The guests are then invited to eat in the dining area. In traditional homes, low tables are placed end to end and laid out with all the dishes that have been prepared for the meal.

A Korean couple in traditional attire treat guests to a large meal.

Before the meal begins, the host will usually tell the guests to eat as much as they want even though the meal is humble. This reflects the Korean belief that even the most sumptuous food is never good enough for honored guests. The host greatly appreciates it if the guests ask for more food, since it is a sign that they are enjoying the food.

However, despite the host's urging to eat a lot, the guests will always leave a little food in their rice bowls at the end of the meal. This serves to assure the host that enough food has been served and the guests have had their fill.

Koreans traditionally do not talk much during meals. Instead, they concentrate on relishing the taste of the food. When the guests have finished, the host will clear the table and serve coffee and seasonal fruit. The host is prepared to entertain the guests for hours, especially when alcohol is served.

ALCOHOLIC DRINKS

Koreans are avid social drinkers. In some areas, it is considered socially unacceptable to drink alcoholic drinks alone. Traditionally, in Korea only men were allowed to drink alcoholic drinks in public, but today women do their fair share of socializing over drinks.

Nonetheless, Koreans follow strict rules when drinking. They never pour alcoholic drinks for themselves but for others. Someone of lower status will offer a glass to someone of higher status, and if the status or age difference is significant, the person receiving the glass as well as the person offering it will either use both hands or hold the glass in the right hand supported by the left. When the glass reaches the receiver's hand, the giver pours the alcohol into it.

It is the custom to pass one's glass on until everyone has exchanged glasses with everyone else. Drinkers do not pour alcohol into a partially filled glass. There is no problem if someone chooses not to drink, but refusing a drink after having started is considered antisocial behavior.

It is considered impolite in Korea to pour your own drink.

129

DONGNAE PAJEON

This savory pancake combines seafood and green onions, which are rich in calcium, iron, and vitamins and are believed to the keep the body warm and ease gastrointestinal functions. This recipe makes 4 pancakes.

½ pound green onions
2 eggs
Pinch of salt
1½ cups water

2 cups flour
½ cup oysters
1 cup clams
6 tablespoons cooking oil

Trim the green onions, cut into 6-inch (15-cm) lengths, and flatten the roots with a knife. Add the eggs and salt to the water, and mix. Add the flour, and mix to form a batter. Wash the oysters and clams in salt water, then drain well and slice into thin strips. Grease a frying pan with a little cooking oil, and heat over low heat. Pour a little batter into the pan, and spread evenly. Spread some of the green onions, oysters, and clams over the batter in the pan, then cover with a little more batter. When the top is slightly firm, press the pancake with a spoon. Cook another 1 to 2 minutes until the underside is properly cooked. Then flip the pancake over, and cook the other side until light brown. Serve warm.

MILGAM HWACHE

This recipe makes a refreshing punch from mandarin oranges, which are vitamin C-rich and help relieve colds and stress.

2 mandarin oranges
1 tablespoon sugar
1 cup sugar
5 cups water
1 tablespoon pine nuts

Peel one of the oranges, and separate the wedges. Sprinkle 1 tablespoon sugar on the wedges. Squeeze the other orange, and set aside the juice. Add 1 cup sugar to the water, and boil. Leave to cool before mixing with the orange juice. Put the sugared wedges in a punch bowl, and pour in the juice and sugar water. Garnish with the pine nuts.

Another after-meal drink, *sujeong-gwa*, uses dried persimmons instead of mandarin oranges. Ginger slices are boiled in water, then cinnamon is added. When the water boils, the ginger and cinnamon are removed. Sugar and more water are added, and the drink is boiled for a while more. Then dried persimmons are added, and the drink is simmered until the persimmons soften.

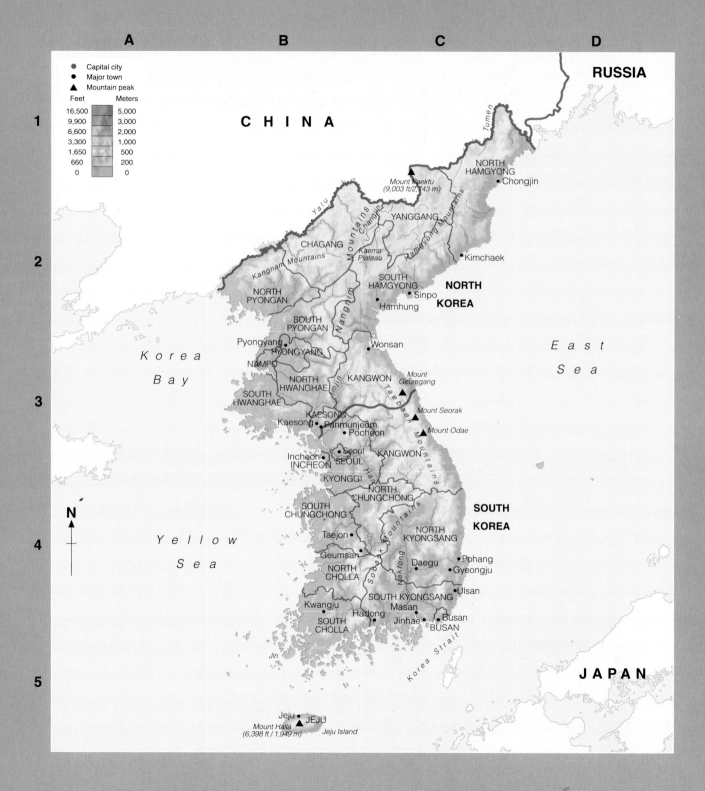

A   **B**   **C**   **D**

● Capital city
● Major town
▲ Mountain peak

Feet	Meters
16,500	5,000
9,900	3,000
6,600	2,000
3,300	1,000
1,650	500
660	200
0	0

1

C H I N A

RUSSIA

Tumen

▲ Mount Paektu
(9,003 ft/2,743 m)

NORTH
HAMGYONG

● Chongjin

Yalu

Changjin

YANGGANG

Kangnyong Mountains

CHAGANG

*Kaema
Plateau*

2

Kangnam Mountains

Nangnim Mountains

SOUTH
HAMGYONG

● Kimchaek

**NORTH
KOREA**

NORTH
PYONGAN

● Sinpo

Hamhung

SOUTH
PYONGAN

*E a s t
S e a*

Pyongyang ●
PYONGYANG

Wonsan ●

NAMPO

*K o r e a
B a y*

NORTH
HWANGHAE

KANGWON

Mount
Geumgang ▲

SOUTH
HWANGHAE

Imjin

Taebaek

3

KAESONG

Mount Seorak ▲

Kaesong ● Panmunjeom
● Pocheon

▲ Mount Odae

Seoul ●
SEOUL

KANGWON

Incheon ●
INCHEON

KYONGGI

Han

Mountains

NORTH
CHUNGCHONG

SOUTH
CHUNGCHONG

**SOUTH
KOREA**

*Yellow
Sea*

Taejon ●

NORTH
KYONGSANG

4

N

Geumsan ●

Daegu ● ● Pohang

● Gyeongju

NORTH
CHOLLA

Sobaek Mountains

Naktong

● Ulsan

Kwangju ●

SOUTH KYONGSANG

Masan ●

Hadong ● Jinhae ● ● Busan
BUSAN

SOUTH
CHOLLA

Korea Strait

Jin

5

J A P A N

Jeju ● ● JEJU
Mount Halla ▲
(6,398 ft / 1,949 m)   *Jeju Island*

MAP OF KOREA

ECONOMIC KOREA

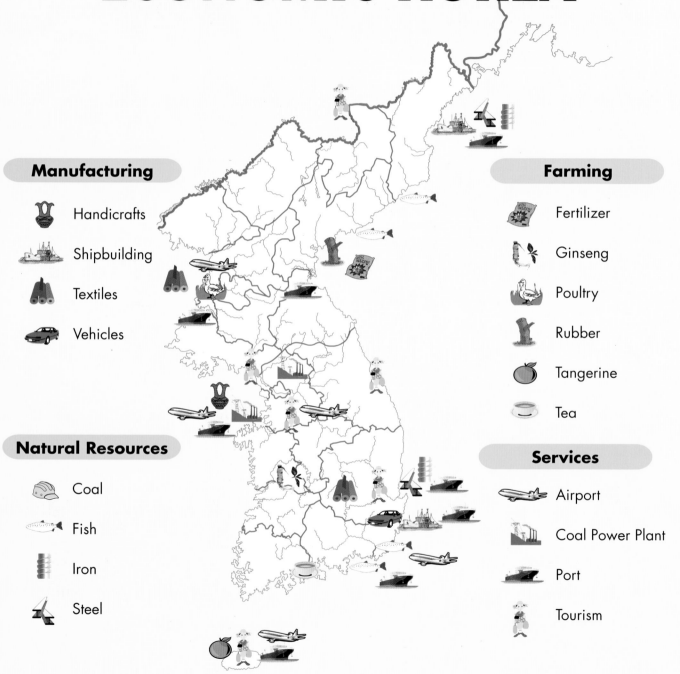

Manufacturing
- Handicrafts
- Shipbuilding
- Textiles
- Vehicles

Natural Resources
- Coal
- Fish
- Iron
- Steel

Farming
- Fertilizer
- Ginseng
- Poultry
- Rubber
- Tangerine
- Tea

Services
- Airport
- Coal Power Plant
- Port
- Tourism

ABOUT THE ECONOMY

OVERVIEW

South Korea's economy grew at high speed in the 1980s, thanks largely to close government and business links. The economy plunged during the Asian financial crisis in the late 1990s but made a strong recovery by 2000. North Korea's economy faces food shortages and poor living conditions. The government spends more on military than civilian needs. International food aid has slowed down since 2003 due to political tensions.

GROSS DOMESTIC PRODUCT (GDP)

South: US$941.5 billion; North: US$22.26 billion (2002 est.)

GDP SECTORS

South: agriculture 8 percent, industry 45 percent, services 47 percent; North: agriculture 30 percent, industry 42 percent, services 28 percent

AGRICULTURAL PRODUCTS

South: barley, cattle, eggs, fish, fruit, milk, pork, poultry, rice, root crops, vegetables; North: cattle, corn, eggs, pork, potatoes, pulses, rice, soybeans

CURRENCY

South Korean won (KRW)
North Korean won (KPW)
USD 1 = KRW 1,157.36 = KPW 2.2 (March 2004)

INDUSTRIAL PRODUCTS

South: clothing, footwear, electronic products, ships, steel, textiles, vehicles; North: metallurgical products, military products, minerals, textiles

WORKFORCE

South: 22 million (agriculture 9.5 percent, industry 21.5 percent, services 69 percent); North: 9.6 million (agriculture 36 percent, others 64 percent)

MAJOR TRADE PARTNERS

South: the United States, Japan, China, North Korea, Hong Kong, Taiwan; North: Japan, China, South Korea, Germany, Russia

MAJOR EXPORTS

South: clothing, footwear, fish, electronic products, ships, steel, textiles, vehicles; North: fish products, metallurgical products, military products, minerals

MAJOR IMPORTS

South: electronic products, grain, oil, organic chemicals, steel, textiles, transportation equipment; North: coking coal, consumer goods, grain, machinery and equipment, petroleum

PORTS

South: Busan, Incheon, Jeju, Jinhae, Masan, Pohang, Ulsan; North: Chongjin, Hamhung, Kimchaek, Nampo, Wonsan

INTERNATIONAL AIRPORTS

South: Incheon, Yangyang, Busan, Jeju; North: Pyongyang

CULTURAL KOREA

Kim Il Sung Square
Pyongyang's center boasts a square similar to China's Tiananmen. Surrounded by important government buildings, Kim Il Sung Square has beautiful views of the Taedong River.

Kaesong
The old capital of the Goryeo dynasty is home to a museum of celadon pottery and other Confucian relics. The city also preserves a traditional Korean atmosphere and natural landscapes such as the Pakyon Falls.

Demilitarized Zone
Panmunjeom is located in the demilitarized zone and is an important venue for peace talks between North and South Korea. Soldiers guard both sides of the border, and civilians need a permit to visit the area.

Ceramics Village
In Incheon, at one of Korea's largest ceramics villages, visitors can buy beautiful quality ceramics as well as learn the art of traditional pottery.

Lake of Heaven
The tallest mountain in the Korean peninsula has a snow-covered peak, or "white head," throughout the year. Mount Paektu's crater contains one of the world's deepest alpine lakes: Cheonji, or Lake of Heaven, up to 1,260 feet (394 m) deep.

Grandfathers of Jeju
Formed from lava deposits, Jeju Island has breathtaking natural volcanic rock structures and more than 40 statues called grandfathers, which are believed to be more than 200 years old.

Mountain Gateway
The Geumgang mountains are home to waterfalls, mineral springs, temples, and a museum. The mountains are the only place where South Koreans can enter North Korea.

Ski Resorts
Both professional and amateur skiers patronize the resorts in Gangwon province from December to March to enjoy South Korea's snowy slopes in winter.

Ancient Palaces
Seoul's five main palaces were built as early as the 15th century. The preserved ruins continue to draw visitors to admire its architecture, gardens, and relics.

Gyeongju
The old capital of the Silla dynasty is known as a museum without walls. Its many well-preserved sites include the ancient tombs of Cheonmachong (Flying Horse Tomb).

ABOUT THE CULTURE

OFFICIAL NAME
South: Republic of Korea; North: Democratic People's Republic of Korea

CAPITAL
South: Seoul; North: Pyongyang

OTHER MAJOR CITIES
South: Busan, Daegu, Incheon, Ulsan; North: Hamhung, Kaesong, Nampo, Wonsan

NATIONAL FLAG
South: white, with black trigrams from the *I Ching* (Book of Changes) and a red and blue yin-yang symbol; North: a red star in a white circle in a red band between two white and two blue stripes.

NATIONAL ANTHEM
South: The Patriotic Hymn. Adopted in 1948. Words by Yun Chi-Io and An Chang-Ho. Music by Ahn Eak-Tae. North: The Patriotic Song. Adopted in 1947. Words by Pak Se-Yong. Music by Kim Won-Gyun.

POPULATION
South: 48,324,000; North: 22,224,195 (2002 est.)

OFFICIAL LANGUAGE
Korean

ETHNIC GROUPS
A large majority of South and North Koreans are ethnic Koreans, while ethnic Chinese make up a small minority in either section of the peninsula.

RELIGIOUS GROUPS
South: Christian 49 percent, Buddhist 47 percent, Confucian 3 percent, other 1 percent; North: non-religious 68 percent, shamanist and Confucian 29.5 percent, Buddhist 1.7 percent, other 0.8 percent

TIME
Greenwich Mean Time plus 9 hours (GMT+0900)

IMPORTANT ANNIVERSARIES
South: Memorial Day (June 6), Liberation Day (August 15); North: Kim Jong Il's birthday (February 16–17), Kim Il Sung's birthday (April 15–16)

LEADERS IN POLITICS
South: Kim Dae Jung (president 1997–2003, Nobel Peace Prize laureate), Roh Moo-Hyun (president since 2003); Koh Kun (prime minister since 2003); North: Kim Jong Il (National Defence Commission chairman and Korean Workers' Party general secretary since 1994); Kim Yong Nam (president of the Supreme People's Assembly's standing committee), Kim Il Sung (prime minister 1948–72, president 1972–94)

OTHER FAMOUS KOREANS
Richard E. Kim (author), Nam June Paik (video artist), Cha Bum Keun (soccer player), Park Se Ri (golfer), Margaret Cho (comedian), Sumi Jo (soprano), and Joseph Hahn (musician)

TIME LINE

IN KOREA	IN THE WORLD
6,000 B.C. Neolithic peoples arrive.	
	753 B.C. Rome is founded.
108 B.C. China's Han dynasty establishes four territories in the peninsula.	**116–17 B.C.** The Roman Empire reaches its greatest extent, under Emperor Trajan (98–17).
57–18 B.C. The Silla, Goguryeo, and Baekje kingdoms are founded.	
	A.D. 600 Height of Mayan civilization
A.D. 668 Goguryeo and Baekje are unified under Silla.	
918 Wang Kon founds Goryeo.	**1000** The Chinese perfect gunpowder and begin to use it in warfare.
1170 Choe Chung-hon establishes military rule.	
1231 Mongols invade Goryeo.	
1392 Yi Seong-gye founds the Joseon dynasty.	**1530** Beginning of trans-Atlantic slave trade organized by the Portuguese in Africa.
1592 Japan invades Korea.	**1558–1603** Reign of Elizabeth I of England
1598 Korea drives out Japan with China's help.	**1620** Pilgrims sail the *Mayflower* to America.
	1776 U.S. Declaration of Independence
	1789–99 The French Revolution
	1861 The U.S. Civil War begins.
	1869 The Suez Canal is opened.
1910 Japan annexes Korea.	**1914** World War I begins.

IN KOREA	IN THE WORLD
	1939 World War II begins.
1945 The peninsula is divided. Soviet troops occupy the north, U.S. troops the south.	**1945** The United States drops atomic bombs on Hiroshima and Nagasaki.
1948 Syngman Rhee is elected president of South Korea; Kim Il Sung leads North Korea.	**1949** The North Atlantic Treaty Organization (NATO) is formed.
1950–53 The Korean War	**1957** The Russians launch Sputnik.
1960–61 Riots force Rhee to resign. Park Chung Hee stages a coup and imposes martial law.	**1966–1969** The Chinese Cultural Revolution
1979 Park is assassinated.	
1988 Seoul hosts the Olympic Games.	**1986** Nuclear power disaster at Chernobyl in Ukraine
1991 Both Koreas join the United Nations.	**1991** Break-up of the Soviet Union
1992 Kim Young Sam introduces political and economic reforms in South Korea. North and South Korea formally agree to denuclearize.	
1994 Kim Jong Il succeeds the late Kim Il Sung.	
1998 Kim Dae Jung engages North Korea with the Sunshine Policy.	**1997** Hong Kong is returned to China.
2000 Kim Dae Jung and Kim Jong Il meet. Families separated by the border reunite. Kim Dae Jung wins the Nobel Peace Prize.	**2001** Terrorists crash planes in New York, Washington, D.C., and Pennsylvania.
2002 South Korea hosts the World Cup.	
2003 North Korea continues its nuclear program in violation of international agreements.	**2003** War in Iraq

GLOSSARY

banchan (bun-CHAHN)
The side dishes that accompany a Korean meal.

chaebol (JAE-bull)
A business conglomerate.

chungmae (choong-MAY)
An arranged marriage.

dol (DOUL)
A child's first birthday.

haenyeo (hay-NIO)
A dwindling group of women divers preserving a more-than-1,500-year-old tradition in Jeju.

ham (HAHM)
A box of gifts for the bride, sent by the groom as part of the Korean wedding ritual.

hanbok (HUN-bok)
The traditional Korean dress.

hangeul (HAHN-gool)
The Korean phonetic writing system.

hwangap (HWUN-gup)
A person's 60th birthday.

insam (in-SUM)
Ginseng, a herb believed to be a cure-all and consumed as a health tonic.

juche (CHOO-cheh)
Self-reliance.

kibun (KEY-boon)
Social harmony.

kimchi (KIM-chee)
A traditional Korean pickle.

kisaeng (KEY-sang)
A female entertainer, usually a talented poet, singer, or musician.

kumjul (KEHM-jool)
A straw rope of chili peppers hung across the doorway of a house to frighten off evil spirits and warn people not to enter because a baby has just been born.

mudang (MOO-dung)
A shaman, or spirit medium.

nunchi (NOON-chi)
An intuition or hunch that enables a person to read another person's state of mind.

ondol (ON-doll)
A system of pipes beneath the floor of a house that carry warm air from the kitchen stove.

Samsin Halmeoni (SUM-sin Hul-MO-neh)
The grandmother spirit associated with childbirth.

Seollal (SUHL-lahl)
The Lunar New Year.

sijo (SAE-jo)
A form of traditional Korean poetry.

FURTHER INFORMATION

BOOKS

Horne, John and Wolfram Manzenreiter (editors). *Japan, Korea and the 2002 World Cup*. New York, NY: Routledge, 2002.

Kim, Jaihiun (translator). *Modern Korean Verse in Sijo Form*. Vancouver, Canada: Ronsdale Press, 1997.

Kim, Minkyoung and J. D. Hilts. *Lonely Planet Korean Phrasebook*. Third Ed. Victoria, Australia: Lonely Planet Publications, 2002.

Lee, Helie. *Still Life With Rice*. New York, NY: Touchstone, 1996.

Lee, Mary Paik. *Quiet Odyssey: A Pioneer Korean Woman in America*. Seattle, WA: University of Washington Press, 1990.

Lee, Peter H. (editor). *The Columbia Anthology of Traditional Korean Poetry*. New York, NY: Columbia University Press, 2002.

Portal, Jane. *Korea: Art and Archaeology*. New York, NY: Thames and Hudson Inc., 2000.

Steers, Richard M. *Made in Korea: Chung Ju Yung and the Rise of Hyundai*. New York, NY: Routledge, 1999.

WEBSITES

Amnesty International Library: North Korea. http://web.amnesty.org/library/eng-prk

BBC News Country Profile: North Korea. http://news.bbc.co.uk/2/hi/asia-pacific/country_profiles/1131421.stm

BBC News Country Profile: South Korea. http://news.bbc.co.uk/2/hi/asia-pacific/country_profiles/1123668.stm

Central Intelligence Agency World Factbook (select North Korea or South Korea in the country list). www.cia.gov/cia/publications/factbook

Korea Baseball Organization (point the mouse on HOME in the main menu and select English). www.koreabaseball.or.kr

Korea National Tourism Organization. www.knto.or.kr/eng

Korean National Heritage Online. www.heritage.go.kr/eng

Korean Overseas Information Service. www.kois.go.kr

Ministry of Environment, Republic of Korea. http://eng.me.go.kr

Official homepage of the Democratic People's Republic of Korea. www.korea-dpr.com

The World Bank Group (type "North Korea" or "South Korea" in the search box). www.worldbank.org

VIDEOS

Families of Korea. Families of the World VHS Series. Master Communications, 2001.

Hidden Korea. PBS Home Video, 2001.

BIBLIOGRAPHY

Farley, Carol. *Land of the Morning Calm*. New York, NY: Macmillan Children's Book Group, 1991.

Macdonald, Donald S. *The Koreans: Contemporary Politics and Society*. Revised edition. Boulder, Colorado: Westview Press, 1990.

Nash, Amy. *North Korea*. New York, NY: Chelsea House, 1991.

Rucci, Richard, B. (editor). American Chamber of Commerce in Korea: *Living In Korea*. Revised edition. Seoul, Korea: Seoul International Tourist Publishing, 1981.

Savada, Andrea Matles. *North Korea: A Country Study*. Washington, D.C.: U.S. Government Printing Office, 1994.

Savada, Andrea Matles. *South Korea: A Country Study*. Washington, D.C.: U.S. Government Printing Office, 1992.

Solberg, Sammy E. *The Land and People of Korea*. New York, NY: Harper Collins, 1991.

South Korea in Pictures. Minneapolis, MN: Department of Geography, Lerner Publications, 1989.

INDEX